Evaluating Vocational Training Programs

Supplied by the
international document
delivery service of

microinfo limited

P.O. BOX 3, NEWMAN LANE,
ALTON, HANTS. GU34 2PG.
ENGLAND
TELEPHONE: 0420-86848
TELEX: 858431 MINFO G

A World Bank Publication

Evaluating Vocational Training Programs

A Practical Guide

Gordon Hunting
Manuel Zymelman
Martin Godfrey

The World Bank
Washington, D.C.

Users of this book are welcome to copy the evaluation forms—tables 1.1 and 4.1 and the materials in the appendixes—or to adapt them to their own needs.

The World Bank does not accept responsibility for the views expressed herein, which are those of the authors and should not be attributed to the World Bank or to its affiliated organizations. The findings, interpretations, and conclusions derive from a project supported by the Bank; they do not necessarily represent official policy of the Bank.

Gordon Hunting is a technical educator in the East Asia and Pacific Regional Office of the World Bank. Manuel Zymelman is a special adviser for the economics of education in Africa for the World Bank. Martin Godfrey is a fellow at the Institute of Development Studies, University of Sussex, United Kingdom.

Library of Congress Cataloging-in-Publication Data

Hunting, Gordon.
   Evaluating vocational training programs.

   1. Technical education—Evaluation. 2. Industrial
arts—Study and teaching—Evaluation. 3. Vocational
education—Evaluation. I. Zymelman, Manuel.
II. Godfrey, Martin. III. Title.
T65.3.H86 1986   607'.1   85-32309
ISBN 0-8213-0703-7

Contents

Preface

This book is the culmination of a journey that started several years ago when experts from multilateral and bilateral aid agencies met to discuss the need to develop a uniform methodology for evaluating industrial training. As a result of this and subsequent meetings, the Agency for Technical Cooperation of the Federal Republic of Germany, the Overseas Development Administration of the United Kingdom, the Swedish International Development Agency, and the World Bank decided to underwrite the cost of producing a comprehensive evaluation guide.

The project required the cooperation of economists, educators, and vocational and technical specialists. We were fortunate to have the advice and help of Peter Sloane, Solomon Cohen, and Gunther Kolheyer during the writing of this manual, and we thank them wholeheartedly. Special recognition should go to Douglas Shaw of the Operational Development Section of the International Labour Organisation, who participated in our mission to Indonesia, where the manual was tested in the field, and who contributed many valuable suggestions to the final version.

We are also grateful to the representatives of multilateral and bilateral agencies who, at a meeting in London in July 1984, discussed a preliminary version of this guide and offered constructive criticism and helpful suggestions.

Introduction

This guide is intended to fill a gap in the resources available for evaluating training programs. The aim is not to write another textbook—with extended definitions of concepts, discussions of their theoretical underpinnings, and references to the literature—or another lengthy cookbook to guide the completely uninitiated reader step by laborious step through every problem and its variations. Rather, it is meant to be a systematic checklist for evaluators of vocational training institutions and for directors of schools or skill centers who want to identify the areas of their own institutions that need improvement.

As with any guide, the type of questions and the data requirements have to be adapted to the specific task at hand and to local conditions. For evaluation of a central training system, more specific questions may be needed; for assessments of in-plant training, many of the suggested questions may be superfluous, and for such problems as comparing the cost-effectiveness of different modes of training, the section on evaluating the efficiency of operations may be omitted or used as background. Although the guide is most useful as a tool for identifying critical points for improving the efficiency of training institutions or systems, it can easily be adapted, in part or as a whole, to all types of evaluations, and its usefulness is not confined to industrial training.

As chapter 1 emphasizes, the approach to the evaluation of a project depends on the purpose of the analysis. For this book we assume that we are engaged in evaluating, from the point of view of society, a training institution that offers pre-career, entirely off-the-job courses.

Diagnosing the efficiency of operations and, in particular, identifying inefficiencies and their causes require both qualitative and quantitative analysis. Chapter 2 explains the use of three checklists and supplementary worksheets (placed at the end of the text as appendixes) for these purposes. Appendix A (the checklist for the qualitative evaluation) provides a format for systematically recording subjective judgments on the key factors in the institution's internal operations. Appendix B (the checklist for the quantitative evaluation) calls for information on resources, costs, and student performance. (Questionnaires and forms for collecting supporting observations and data for these checklists are in appendixes D and E.) Although our main concern is with individual institutions, we have also included, in appendix C, a checklist and forms for describing the policies and procedures of the responsible central agency that affect the institution.

The checklists can be used not only for formal evaluations but also for periodic in-house assessments by school management. The user is free to adapt the checklists and worksheets to the particular occasion and institution. For example, if a school is using the checklists for its own evaluations, not all the supporting material in appendixes D and E will have to be collected anew each time. And whether or not a school undertakes regular self-evaluations, administrators may find that many of the worksheets are useful for keeping running records of operations.

Chapter 3 describes methods for assessing costs and outcomes in order to evaluate external efficiency—the effectiveness with which an institution fulfills its purpose. The literature on the subject emphasizes quantitative assessment—increased earnings of graduate trainees, employment rates of graduates, and so on. This chapter discusses extensively various cost-outcome measures but also makes the point that many outcomes are not easily quantified and that observations and interviews are important aids in interpreting the quantitative data. Examples of questionnaires that might be used to interview employers and former students concerning the value of the training are provided in appendix F. Because the indicators described in this chapter would be collected by outside evaluators rather than by schools, we have gone into less detail in this chapter than in that on efficiency of operations. Nevertheless, the purposely concise discussion of measures of effectiveness should be of interest to school administrators, and the examples of questionnaires may be useful in the school's own program of following up the employment experience of graduates.

Chapter 4 presents a compact format for summarizing results of the evaluation, using a numeric scale that can be used to compare several institutions as well as to identify the strengths and weaknesses of particular institutions. In addition, it suggests concrete procedures for conducting an evaluation, provides a sample timetable, and discusses issues that have to be considered in drawing up and administering questionnaires.

Throughout this guide we stress that an evaluation is much more than a series of cardinal measurements that somehow can be manipulated to yield a single figure on an efficiency scale. An evaluation also must include the impressions and qualitative assessments of experts whose experience provides a solid basis for judgment. It is hoped that the gestalt approach suggested here, which permits the blending of quantitative indicators with informed judgments, will be a further step toward the development of a comprehensive evaluation methodology.

Defining the Purpose of the Evaluation

Project evaluation involves the ex-post analysis of the functioning, outcomes, and costs of a project. If the evaluation is done as part of midterm monitoring, it will focus on ways of improving the project (for example, by redesigning its mode, curricula, or management) or perhaps on decisions about its continuation, expansion, or replication. If it comes at the end of a project, it will be mainly concerned with the project's success or failure and with drawing lessons applicable to subsequent projects.

The nature of the project is important to evaluation. Are we looking at a training system as a whole, a training institution, or a course? If at a course, is it intended for precareer training or for upgrading? Is it short or long? Off-the-job or on-the-job? The objectives of the project also affect our approach. Are the objectives defined in terms of efficiency, in one sense or another, or of equity? Finally, we need to know from whose viewpoint the analysis is being conducted.

The Nature of the Project

Evaluating a single precareer course that is entirely off-the-job is a straightforward type of project analysis. Here it is relatively easy to isolate costs and benefits. In the case of a course intended to upgrade skills, workers' performance before and after training may be measured. Evaluating on-the-job training is more difficult because of questions of costing that require special treatment.

Analysis of an entire training institution (unless it offers only one course) is inevitably more complex than evaluating single courses. Many institutions offer courses in a bewildering variety of subject matter, length, skill level (initial or upgrading), format (on- or off-the-job, full-time or part-time), and purpose (vocational or nonvocational). In such cases analysis of the demand-supply situation has to cover a wide range of occupations, and outcome-cost analysis, whether concerned with external or with internal efficiency, has to be disaggregated to the level of the individual course. The same is true of analysis of a whole system, unless it consists of only one mode. Thus, evaluation of, say, an on-the-job apprenticeship system can be conducted at an aggregate level, but evaluation of a system that includes several routes has to be disaggregated.

The Objectives of the Project

The criteria used by a project analyst obviously depend on the objectives of the project, but identifying these can be difficult. Projects often have multiple, sometimes conflicting, objectives. Most projects aim at being efficient, in the sense of achieving the highest possible outcome-cost ratio, but efficiency has several dimensions.

Efficiency can be defined in terms of academic performance—which may not be fully measurable by test or examination scores, including as it does increases in skills, changes in attitudes, cognitive development, and acquisition of knowledge. We need to know who is supposed to learn what, under what conditions, and by what date.

Efficiency also can be defined in terms of skill on the job after graduation. Measurement of a project's impact in this respect will not be easy in any case, but it will be impossible unless we know what the project was trying to achieve.

Another dimension of efficiency is productivity and income in employment, which may or may not vary directly with the degree of skill acquired by the trainee.

In projects that are not oriented toward the labor market efficiency may be particularly difficult to define. Gains in academic achievement or acquisition of skill may be among the results, but the project may also have important, not easily measured, effects on the morale or well-being of the participants. (Adult literacy classes are an example.)

Finally, a project's efficiency may be defined partly in terms of its indirect or spillover effects, such as a change in the role of women or the wider impact on the labor market of changes in the supply of skills.

For some projects success is measured in terms of their impact on equity. Their objective is to improve the relative position of a given underprivileged group with respect to any or all of the effects discussed above.

Whatever the objectives of a project, the analyst needs to have them clearly set out before he can select his criteria for evaluation. Where there are multiple objectives, and particularly if they conflict, it may be necessary for him to assign weights to them to arrive at an overall assessment.

The Point of View

The criteria used in the analysis also depend on the viewpoint that is adopted. Are we looking at the project from the point of view of the nation, or of society as a whole (the most usual practice)? From the narrower budgetary point of view of the government or the treasury? Or from the perspective of the aid agency involved in financing the project, the local community, or the firm that sponsors a trainee or an individual student? Taking any of these viewpoints can be useful for different purposes, and each implies a variation in method.

The Initial Checklist

In order to be clear about the purpose of a project analysis, it is useful to fill out an initial checklist (table 1.1). In the following chapters we will assume, for purposes of exposition, that we have checked the following items: A.2, B.1.b, B.2.a,

B.3.a, B.4.a, C.1.a–c, D.1. In other words, we assume that we are conducting an evaluation of a training institution that offers long-term precareer, entirely-off-the-job courses; that the project's objectives include efficiency in all except the non-labor-market and spillover senses; and that we are appraising it from the point of view of society as a whole.

Table 1.1. *Initial Checklist: Purpose of Project*
Instructions: Check appropriate box.

A. Stage of evaluation	
1. Midterm	☐
2. Final	☐
3. Other (regular or periodic)	☐
B. Description of project	
1. Scope	
a. Whole system	☐
b. Multicourse training institution	☐
c. Single course training institution	☐
d. Single course	☐
2. Length of training	
a. Long (more than three months)	☐
b. Short (up to three months)	☐
3. Focus	
a. Precareer	☐
b. Upgrading	☐
4. Mode	
a. Entirely off-the-job	☐
b. Entirely on-the-job	☐
c. Mixed	☐
C. Project objectives	
1. Efficiency	
a. Academic performance	☐
b. Skill on the job	☐
c. Productivity in employment	☐
d. Non-labor-market	☐
e. Spillover	☐
2. Equity	☐
D. Point of view	
1. Nation or society	☐
2. Treasury	☐
3. Aid agency	☐
4. Local community	☐
5. Firm	
6. Individual student	☐

Evaluating the Efficiency of Operations

This chapter deals with the efficiency of operations (the internal efficiency) of a technical school or vocational training center. It examines the main aspects of internal operations, including the content and relevance of the courses, the teaching methods, the quality of the staff, the adequacy and utilization of space, the appropriateness and use of equipment, the effectiveness of management, and the interrelations with industry.

Evaluation of the efficiency of operations (accompanied by an understanding of the underlying factors) is a powerful management tool, both for the director or principal of the school and for the ministry or agency responsible for supervising the institution. It is particularly important when a system or institution is being expanded or when measurements of external efficiency indicate deficiencies in the system that call for improvements in operations. Evaluation also provides a basis for comparing the performance of different institutions.

Assessing efficiency, and in particular identifying inefficiencies and their causes, require subjective judgment as well as quantitative analysis. The diagnosis must be carried out by an experienced technical educator, and it requires the full involvement and cooperation of the senior staff of the institution concerned.

The process of evaluation starts with identification of the key factors that are commonly recognized as being of primary importance in determining the efficiency of a system. In this chapter we identify those key factors and describe how they are assessed through the use of checklists, questionnaires, and other means.

A training program can be judged only after observing the teaching process, including practical laboratory and workshop activities, to assess the method and quality of instruction. Examination results provide data for the quantitative study of internal efficiency, but the quality of the examinations administered and the relevance of examination methods to the training must also be assessed. The source and quality of students and trainees and the processes by which they are selected and counseled at entry and assisted to find appropriate employment after training ends should also be evaluated.

An important factor in determining efficiency is the quantity and quality of teaching staff. The evaluation team will need to look at the procedures for selection, appointment, assignment, and promotion of staff, as well as their salaries and other conditions of service. The quality of staff is assessed and deficiencies and training needs are identified by studying personnel records that show qualifications and experience and by observing teachers' performance, the quality of the teaching programs and materials, and the students' work. The utilization and performance of support personnel, particularly laboratory and workshop employees and professional staff such as librarians, must also be evaluated.

The quality and effectiveness of training can be affected significantly by the adequacy and utilization of physical resources (buildings, equipment, and materials). Overprovision and underutilization are as inefficient as underprovision, with its consequent overcrowding and inadequate facilities. Here, as for the other key factors, the evaluation team must weigh carefully the quantitative and qualitative assessments. Facilities can be measured in unit areas of teaching space or unit costs of equipment; the actual utilization of space or equipment can be compared with the maximum theoretical use to yield utilization factors. For each quantitative measure there are broad values or norms that are accepted internationally as good practice. However, it must be kept in mind that an apparently adequate quantitative figure may conceal inefficient or ineffective procedures. For example, a reasonable average level of utilization (say, 75 percent for workshops) may represent extreme overcrowding for part of the time and zero use for the remainder. Workshops and equipment may be in use most of the time, but the training exercises and activities may be of poor quality. The expenditure on equipment may be reasonable, but the equipment may be inappropriate for the objectives of the training program.

The effectiveness of the school's management is evaluated by examining the organizational structure and the management style and effectiveness of the senior staff. The latter can be judged only qualitatively, but that judgment will be illuminated by the evaluation of other key factors; that is, good or poor ratings in such areas as utilization of facilities are part of the supporting data for judging management effectiveness.

The interrelationship of the training institution with industry is probably the most important single indicator of its efficiency and effectiveness. This interrelationship can be measured in terms of employment of trainees, formal links between the institution and industry, the staff's industrial experience and connections, and the extent to which the institution engages in production or other practical activities and creates an environment similar to that of industry. (These measures overlap with some used in determining external efficiency.)

Normally, a training center or school is part of a vocational training or technical education system and is responsible to a government organization such as the ministry of labor, manpower, or education. The system may impose constraints or conditions that have a major influence on the operations of the institution. For example, in an extremely centralized system in which curricula, courses, and training materials are developed centrally, teachers are recruited and appointed centrally, and all materials are procured and distributed from a central office, there may be little scope for the school or center to control its own efficiency. It is therefore necessary in any evaluation to look at relevant aspects of the national system.

We have mentioned costs only incidentally, since they are normally included under external efficiency. However, patterns and levels of expenditure on training activities—not just raw numbers—should be taken into account in evaluating operations. For example, a comparison of cost-effectiveness of two similar training institutions could give misleading indications of effectiveness if one center achieved lower costs over the short term by, for example, failing to replace equipment or restock consumable materials, or neglecting maintenance. The checklists and worksheets include questions designed to identify satisfactory or unsatisfactory budgetary practices.

The Qualitative Evaluation

Experience has shown that certain key factors, summarized in the outline below, have a primary influence on the overall efficiency of an institution. The checklist in appendix A (supported by appendixes D and E) uses these factors as a systematic basis for guiding the evaluation team in making value judgments on the quality of the institution's operations. Those judgments must be made by experienced technical educators and must take into account the environment and objectives of the project, as described in chapter 1. The goal is to build up a profile that shows the state of health of the institution with respect to each key factor so that deficiencies can be identified and the scope and nature of remedial action can be determined.

Level, Content, Quality, and Relevance of the Training Program

- The format and content of the curricula and syllabuses
- The implementation of the courses: the teaching process, methods, materials used, and training activities
- The examination scheme; content and conduct of examinations

Students

- Selection methods, entry qualifications, and sponsorship
- Counseling, guidance, placement, and follow-up
- Student-staff relationships

Staffing and Staff Development

- Staffing policy, salaries, and other conditions of service
- Selection and qualifications of staff
- Size and quality of staff; turnover
- Size, quality, and salaries of support staff
- Staff development plans; training (pre-service and in-service)

Physical Resources

- Range, areas, and layout of accommodations
- Facilities, services, and maintenance
- Range, relevance, and adequacy of equipment
- Equipment use, maintenance, and repair
- Replacement and updating of equipment
- Use, replacement, and storage of consumable materials

Organization and Management

- Institutional development plan and objectives
- Organizational structure and responsibilities
- Management information system: availability and use
- Management style and effectiveness

Interrelations with Industry

- Training and employment
- Formal links and services
- Industrial links of staff
- Industry-like environment

The Quantitative Evaluation

Quantitative indicators of efficiency of operations include student flow rates and performance, staff load, provision and utilization of facilities and resources, and breakdowns of training costs. The evaluation team uses the checklist in appendix B, backed up by appendixes D and E, to record this information.

Student Flow Rates

The most useful measures of student flow are

- *Admission rate* (the proportion of applicants admitted to the course)
- *Dropout rate* (the number of students who leave during the course without taking final tests or examinations, as a proportion of students enrolled at the beginning of the course)
- *Repetition rate* (the number of students who repeat a stage of training as a proportion of the students enrolled in that stage in the previous year)
- *Pass rate* (the number of students completing the course successfully as a proportion of the students enrolled in the final year or stage of the course).

Student Performance (Efficiency Indexes)

An overall indicator of internal efficiency in terms of student performance is found by dividing the number of graduates by the number of students entering at the beginning of the course to yield a percentage. If the amount of repetition is significant, however, it is more useful to employ a measure that indicates how much additional time over the planned time is required to produce graduates. Examples are

- Average time required to produce a graduate (total student-years spent on training (including time spent by dropouts) divided by number of graduates produced; this can then be compared with planned time
- Output-input ratio (the number of graduates, multiplied by planned course length in years, as a proportion of the total number of student-years spent in training).

Staffing

Indicators include

- Student-teacher ratio (by course or for the institution)
- Average class size (preferably separately for classroom work and laboratory or workshop activities)

• Average teacher workload (normally expressed as teaching hours or contact hours per week).

Facility Schedules and Utilization of Space

Indicators include

• Average area of workspace (area of classrooms, or laboratories, or workshops, divided by the normal working capacity)
• Average areas of support spaces (area of library, communal spaces, living accommodations, and the like divided by number of students using each kind of area)
• Space utilization (the actual student occupancy of total teaching space as a proportion of the total capacity of the teaching space).

Costs

The most important cost measure is the cost per student per year or cost per graduate. Other analyses of cost also provide valuable comparative data:

• Staff salaries as proportion of total cost
• Cost per student per year for consumable materials
• Maintenance cost as proportion of capital costs.

The Central Training System

The section deals with methods for evaluating the main aspects of the central government training system to gain an understanding of the context within which the training institution operates. Such an evaluation can also provide the basis for a study of the technical and vocational education system as a whole. Appendix C provides a format for recording observations and data.

The key factors in evaluating the central system are

• Policies, planning, and development
• Central and regional control
    Training programs and courses
    Staffing
    Physical resources
    Finances
    Management organization

3

Evaluating External Efficiency

Conceivably, an institution could be extremely efficient internally—making good use of staff and physical resources and achieving a high ratio. of graduates to entrants—and yet turn out graduates who fared no better in the workplace than untrained workers. External efficiency—how well the institution fulfills its stated purposes—is the subject of this chapter. Much of the information needed for assessing external efficiency—costs, outcomes, and their relation—can be expressed quantitatively. As in the analysis of efficiency of operations, however, informed judgment is essential in determining what kind of information is pertinent and what weight should be given to the various indicators.

Cost

How cost is defined depends on the point of view from which the project is being appraised. Since in this case we are taking the point of view of society as a whole, we are interested in the *social opportunity cost* of the project: what will society have to give up to build and operate this training institution? If we were looking at it from a narrower point of view—that of an individual, a local community, or even the treasury—we would still be interested in opportunity cost, but from that particular viewpoint.

The first step in calculating the cost of a project is to analyze from project documents and audited accounts the costs incurred during the gestation of the project—costs of planning, preparation, land value, construction, and equipment. These are *capital items* that depreciate over the lifetime of the project. Since tying up capital also means forgoing an annual return that could have been obtained by using that capital in another way, it is usual to multiply the cost of capital investment by an annualization factor that reflects both depreciation over the lifetime of the item and the return to the capital in an alternative use (that is, the social rate of discount, which is not necessarily the same as the official interest rate). The annualization factor (a) for any given expected service life (n) and social rate of discount (r) is given by the formula

$$a_{r,n} = \frac{r(1+r)^n}{(1+r)^n - 1}.$$

Values of the annualization factor for each expected service life and social rate of discount are found in table 3.1. If, for example, the price of a piece of workshop

Table 3.1. *Values of the Annualization Factor*

	r (percent)				
n	0	5	7.5	10	15
1	1.000	1.000	1.000	1.000	1.000
2	0.500	0.538	0.557	0.576	0.615
3	0.333	0.367	0.385	0.402	0.438
4	0.250	0.282	0.299	0.315	0.350
5	0.200	0.231	0.247	0.264	0.298
6	0.167	0.197	0.213	0.230	0.264
7	0.143	0.173	0.189	0.205	0.240
8	0.125	0.155	0.171	0.187	0.223
9	0.111	0.141	0.157	0.174	0.210
10	0.100	0.130	0.146	0.163	0.199
11	0.091	0.120	0.137	0.154	0.191
12	0.083	0.113	0.129	0.147	0.184
13	0.077	0.106	0.123	0.141	0.179
14	0.071	0.101	0.118	0.136	0.175
15	0.067	0.096	0.113	0.131	0.171
20	0.050	0.080	0.098	0.117	0.160
25	0.040	0.071	0.090	0.110	0.155
50	0.020	0.055	0.077	0.101	0.150

Note: n, service life in years; *r*, social rate of discount.

equipment is $10,000 and its expected service life is 13 years, at a social rate of discount of 10 percent the annualization factor is 0.141 and the annual cost is $1,410.

The second step is to calculate the *recurrent costs* involved in the operation of the project: costs of teaching, training, administrative, and service staff; costs of materials, tools, books, maintenance, and replacement; costs of utilities; and costs for travel, consultants' services, medical services, insurance, and so on. In a situation in which prices change because of inflation, a price adjustment must be made so that costs will be in constant values. Where there is a physical input that involves no payment, such as the services of volunteer workers and teachers and even the time of the trainees themselves (if society is losing their output as a result of their participation in the project), we should assign to these services an opportunity cost in terms of forgone earnings. (These may admittedly be zero if no alternative opportunity for the use of that time exists.)

In some cases we also have to adjust for differences between market price and *social opportunity cost*, or shadow price. For example, from the point of view of society, as opposed to that of an individual, a tax on a piece of equipment should not be counted as a cost; similarly, a subsidy to a particular input reduces its price but not its social cost. So, taxes of all kinds should be deducted from the price of inputs, and subsidies should be added to that price. Also, if there is widespread unemployment or underemployment, so that labor can be withdrawn from an alternative use without much affecting output, the social cost of the labor is likely to be lower than its wage. If there is no active land market, the rent paid may understate the social cost of using a piece of land for the project; some estimate then has to be made of the returns that could be obtained from using the land in the best alternative way. Finally, if foreign exchange is undervalued (as indicated by a chronic balance of payments deficit and lack of foreign exchange reserves), imported inputs have to be valued at a price higher than the market price.

In this way it is possible to put together a year-by-year stream of costs adjusted for inflation and, if necessary, for differences between market price and social cost. Time series of costs by type of expenditure can be compared with costs of other similar institutions. An analysis of the trends of the level and structure of costs can also indicate future tendencies.

Outcome

Outcomes of a training project are assessed at different times and using different measures. *Educational* outcome can be measured at the end of the training period; application of *skills* and impact on *development* can be evaluated only after the trainee has returned to the workplace. Information on these latter types of outcome can be difficult to obtain. Follow-up studies of graduates provide data for only the first years of work life. Government statistical agencies may conduct regular, general surveys of employment and earnings, but they are likely to be highly aggregated and confined to the modern sector. Surveys of private sector salaries (sometimes carried out by private consulting firms) and of civil service salary scales may be of some use. Ways of supplementing these sources through direct observation and interviews are discussed below.

In measuring educational outcome we are interested first in knowing or estimating the success rate (the ratio of a given cohort of graduates from the final year of the course to the number who entered in the first year). The success rate reflects not only the pass rate in the final examination but also dropouts and repetition of course work and examinations by students; information on all these phenomena is useful. In addition, more sensitive measures of educational outcome are desirable. Ideally, the analyst will want to observe the learning process, hold discussions with students and teachers, and perhaps administer his own tests to measure the educational gains made by the trainees in comparison either with their own pretraining scores or with the scores of a control group similar to them in every respect except exposure to this form of training. These test results could be compared with results of external examinations. For example, examination results in institutions that take the program's graduates can be surveyed for evidence of the program's impact on the graduates' performance, compared with performance of trainees from other backgrounds. Examination and test results are often collected and analyzed by the responsible ministries. There may, indeed, be a government department or agency that is primarily concerned with the internal efficiency of training institutions and carries out regular surveys of examination systems, teaching methods, performance, and attitudes. In some countries results of government trade tests of craft skills can be a useful guide to the educational outcome of craft training. Directors of institutions that feed into the program being evaluated or of those that take the program's graduates can also provide useful information and comments.

For skill and development outcomes, the most promising source of information is probably the workplace. ("Workplace" should be interpreted broadly to include informal as well as formal places of work and such places of "nonwork" and job-seeking as marketplaces, factory gates, and official and unofficial employment exchanges. Managers of exchanges, as well as job-seekers, are useful sources of information.) What difference does the specific type of training make in the skill with which trainees do their jobs as compared with either their pretraining level of skill or with a control group? Again, personal observation by the analyst is the ideal method, but since this is usually not possible, it is necessary to fall back on indicators of physical productivity (for example, gross value of yield per acre in agriculture, the time taken to do a particular job compared with the norm estimated by management, the number of errors, or the scrap rate) or on the opinions of work supervisors.

Employers' opinions about the effectiveness of the program should be sought through questionnaires and interviews and, if possible, in the form of ratings of individual on-the-job performance. Employers can also provide factual information on the jobs and on wages and salaries of persons from different training backgrounds. Managers and supervisors can provide similar information and may be particularly useful in rating performance. The workers themselves can tell us about their age, trade, education and training, nature of current job, social background, and job and wage history since joining the labor force. (Examples of questionnaires for employers and employees are given in appendix F.)

For obtaining information on posttraining history, the most scientific method is undoubtedly the tracer project, which attempts to follow, often at regular intervals, a cohort from a particular training institution. Preferably, a number of parallel studies are carried out; this permits a comparison of the posttraining history of cohorts from different educational or training backgrounds. The problem with this method is that it is extremely expensive, particularly in a large country, and relies heavily on enumerators who have to demonstrate extraordinary qualities of ingenuity, honesty, and persistence if the studies are to be successful. Once members of the cohort are traced, a questionnaire can be administered to them. Alternatively, as a shortcut, an extended questionnaire can be administered to a sizable sample of the labor force, both employed and unemployed. The sample may be random or selective; in the latter case, care is taken to include certain categories—firms representing different sizes, locations, and sectors, firms on the books of the employment exchange, and so on. The purpose of the survey is to determine whether there is any measurable difference in labor market experience between persons from different educational and training backgrounds. The same sample of firms could be used to survey employers, managers, and supervisors, using the questionnaire as a basis but carrying out the survey by interview.

Since the ultimate aim of any project is to contribute to development, this is the most important dimension of outcome. Unfortunately, it is also the most difficult to measure. The usual practice is to use as a measure of benefit earnings—or, more precisely, the difference that the training makes to the lifetime earnings stream of those who undergo it. The difference is measured in relation either to what they could have expected without this training or to the expected lifetime earnings stream of a control group. This raises formidable problems of data. We need to know existing earnings patterns for workers of different ages, with and without such training, and the probability of their having jobs, and to guess how these patterns and probabilities will evolve over a period of thirty years or more. How far, for instance, will the increase in the number of trained people itself reduce differentials between the more and the less trained?

There are also conceptual problems. The use of earnings as a measure of benefit is derived from the marginal productivity theory of wages whereby a profit-maximizing employer will not expand his work force if an extra worker would add more to his costs than to his revenue. In a perfectly competitive labor market, the wage is equal to productivity at the margin; hence the use of wages or earnings to measure productivity or benefit. However, the profit-maximizing calculus does not apply to all employers. The public sector, for instance, has quite different objectives, and some adjustment of public sector wages may be necessary for our purposes. And if, as is often the case, labor markets are not perfectly competitive, the wage will be lower than marginal productivity even in the profit-maximizing sector.

Even if earnings broadly reflect productivity, there are important indirect effects that are not captured by this measure and that have to be taken into account.

First, on completion of their courses trainees may be placed in jobs that were held by others up to that point or may fill vacancies that would have been filled by others in the absence of the training scheme (the displacement effect). In the extreme case in which a trained worker merely bumps a less trained worker out of a job, taking over but not increasing the lifetime earnings stream associated with that job, the net social benefit from the training is zero.

Second, there may also be a replacement effect if the slot in the labor market vacated by the worker who joins a training scheme and subsequently moves into a higher occupational category is filled by another worker who would otherwise have remained unemployed. This should be counted as an extra benefit.

Third is the demonstration effect, whereby the skills acquired by trainees are diffused to others who have not undergone the training. This indirect effect can be quantitatively important, particularly in rural areas or among the urban self-employed.

Fourth, training may have important social effects that later yield economic benefits. For instance, training women may be important in reducing the fertility level.

Fifth, by breaking bottlenecks, training may have important dynamic effects not captured by the increase in earnings of the individual trainee. The resulting increase in output may open up employment opportunities for complementary workers who would otherwise be unemployed. And the creation of a pool of skilled labor may be an important factor in attracting more advanced technology to an economy, leading to a higher rate of growth in the future.

Enough has been said to suggest that earnings differentials are at best a partial and at worst a misleading measure of the impact on development of a training program. The list below summarizes the steps in the analysis of the impact on development of a training program. At each stage quantification should be taken as far as possible. But giving a qualitative answer to a question (indicating the direction in which quantities should be modified) is always better than pretending that the question does not exist.

1. Estimate year by year the lifetime earnings stream of an average trainee after completion of the training being evaluated, taking into account the probability of employment.
2. Estimate the expected lifetime earnings stream of an average trainee if he or she had not undergone this training, or of an average member of a control group similar in every other respect except exposure to this training.
3. Deduct (2) from (1) to derive the average differential in lifetime streams of earnings attributable to this program.
4. Adjust (3) downward if trainees are destined for an apparently overmanned part of the public sector, upward if for a part that is undermanned or overworked; upward if for an imperfect private sector labor market.
5. Adjust (3) upward if the replacement effect appears to be important.

6. Adjust (3) upward if the demonstration effect appears to be important.
7. Adjust (3) upward or downward to reflect net social effects.
8. Adjust (3) upward if the effect in breaking bottlenecks appears to be important.

Comparing Cost and Outcome

The simplest cost-outcome calculations are those that combine cost with not necessarily comparable outcomes in unit cost measures. For example, expenditure on plant and equipment for a proposed institution divided by the maximum number of students that can be enrolled in that institution at full capacity yields capital cost per student place. This allows comparisons among different projects (say, a polytechnical institution and a university) or different methods of building and equipping a given project. If capital costs are annualized as described above, capital and current costs can be combined as total cost per student or per graduate, which again allows comparisons among different projects or different ways of building and running a given project (for example, with more or fewer teachers per student). Cost per student raises no problems, being merely total cost over any time period divided by the number of students undergoing training in that period. Cost per graduate is slightly more complicated because estimates of the rates of dropout, repetition, and examination failure are needed.

Cost per graduate can be calculated using the equation

$$Cg = \frac{u\, \Sigma_t^{t-1}\, C + v\, \Sigma_t^{t-2}\, C + \cdots n\, \Sigma_t^{t-m}\, C + s\, \Sigma_t^{t-1}\, C + w\, \Sigma_t^{t-2}\, C + \cdots n\, \Sigma_t^{t-m}\, C}{g}$$

where Cg is cost per graduate in year t; C is average cost per student per year; g is number of graduates in year t; $u, v, \ldots, n$ are groups of graduates in year t classified according to number of years spent in training; and $s, w, \ldots, n$ are groups of dropouts and examination failures in year t classified according to number of years spent in training. As can be seen, use of the cost-per-graduate measure implies assigning a zero valuation to dropouts and examination failures, which may not be justified.

Where it is difficult to assign a money value to the outcome of a project, a cost-effectiveness measure is often used. If there is a scale of possible outcomes (as, say, in the case of examination scores), we can calculate the cost per unit of the appropriate measure. For instance, if there is a choice between three types of training institutions, each offering a similar one-year course but differing in the quality of intake and in final examination marks, the cost-effectiveness comparison can be made as in the example below.

	Total cost per student per year (dollars)	Average score on entry (percent)	Final examination score (percent)	Effectiveness measure (change in score, in percentage points)	Cost ÷ effectiveness measure
Project A	600	40	60	20	30
Project B	375	50	65	15	25
Project C	350	60	70	10	35

Project B is the most cost effective in terms of least dollars spent per percentage point gained per student, even though project A is more effective and project C is less costly. The problem with comparisons of this kind is that they are based on the assumptions that percentage gains in scores (say, 40 to 60) are equally valuable all along the scale, and that other things are equal. From this point of view it would have been safer to compare projects with similar average scores on entry; but the decisionmaker still has to decide the marginal utility of a percentage gain in scores.

Where it is possible to attach money values to the outcome, some kind of cost-benefit calculation can be attempted. The most widely used approaches are to calculate the benefit-cost ratio or the net present value of the internal rate of return. Whichever approach is chosen, we start with the stream of costs (listed in the years that they occur) over the project's lifetime and the stream of benefits emanating from the project over the lifetimes of those who emerge from it (see "Cost" and "Outcome," above) and calculate the discounted present value of both streams. This must be done because resources have alternative uses. If, instead of being used for the project under consideration, $1 were invested elsewhere in the economy, it would yield an annual return at the social rate of discount and so in several years would have grown to much more than $1. By the same reasoning we would be willing to offer less than $1 now for the promise of $1 (at constant prices) some time in the future—how much less again depends on the social rate of discount. This present value of a future payment is known as the discounted present value and is given by the equation $PV = FV/(1+r)^t$, where PV is present value in year 1 of the project, FV is future value, r is the social rate of discount, and t is the number of years hence. Table 3.2 shows the present value of a $1 payment made or received a given number of years in the future at a given social rate of discount. For instance, $1 to be paid thirteen years hence would be worth $0.29 today if the social rate of discount were 10 percent.

Once we have calculated, with the aid of such a present value table, the discounted present value of the stream of costs (C) and the discounted present value of the stream of benefits (B), the rest is easy. The benefit-cost ratio is simply B/C, and the net present value of the project is $B - C$. Thus, where for a particular project at a social discount rate of 10 percent $B = \$250,000$ and $C = \$200,000$, the benefit-cost ratio is 1.25 and the net present value is $50,000. On either count, since the benefit-cost ratio exceeds one and the net present value exceeds zero, it is worthwhile to proceed with the project.

Because such results are sensitive to the social rate of discount chosen, some analysts prefer to calculate an internal rate of return. This is defined as the discount rate at which the present value of the stream of benefits is exactly equal to the present value of the stream of costs. In equation form this is given by

$$\sum_{t=0}^{n} \frac{C_t}{(1+r)^t} = \sum_{t=0}^{n} \frac{B_t}{(1+r)^t}.$$

The most practical way of calculating the internal rate or return is by trial and error, calculating present values for successive assumptions about discount rate, which brings the two sides of the equation closer together.

Whenever possible, the results of cost-benefit calculations should be subjected to sensitivity analysis to test their sensitivity to changes in assumptions, for example, about the impact of the project on earnings differentials or, in the case of the benefit-cost ratio and net present value approaches, about the social rate of discount. Also, when the information available about cost and benefits is inadequate, a range of cost-benefit calculations can be made on plausible assumptions about likely maxi-

Table 3.2. *Discounted Present Value of a $1 Future Payment* t

			r *(percent)*			
t	3	5	8	10	12	15
1	0.9709	0.9524	0.9259	0.9091	0.8929	0.8696
2	0.9426	0.9070	0.8573	0.8264	0.7972	0.7561
3	0.9151	0.8638	0.7938	0.7513	0.7118	0.6575
4	0.8885	0.8227	0.7350	0.6830	0.6355	0.5718
5	0.8626	0.7835	0.6806	0.6209	0.5674	0.4972
6	0.8675	0.7462	0.6302	0.5645	0.5066	0.4323
7	0.8131	0.7107	0.5835	0.5132	0.4523	0.3759
8	0.7894	0.6768	0.5403	0.4665	0.4039	0.3269
9	0.7664	0.6446	0.5002	0.4241	0.3606	0.2843
10	0.7441	0.6139	0.4632	0.3855	0.3220	0.2472
11	0.7224	0.5847	0.4289	0.3505	0.2875	0.2149
12	0.7014	0.5568	0.3970	0.3186	0.2566	0.1869
13	0.6810	0.5305	0.3677	0.2897	0.2292	0.1625
14	0.6611	0.5010	0.3405	0.2633	0.2046	0.1413
15	0.6419	0.4810	0.3152	0.2394	0.1827	0.1229
16	0.6232	0.4581	0.2919	0.2176	0.1631	0.1069
17	0.6050	0.4363	0.2703	0.1978	0.1456	0.0929
18	0.5874	0.4155	0.2502	0.1799	0.1300	0.0808
19	0.5703	0.3957	0.2317	0.1635	0.1161	0.0703
20	0.5537	0.3769	0.2145	0.1486	0.1037	0.0611
21	0.5675	0.3589	0.1987	0.1351	0.0926	0.0531
22	0.5219	0.3418	0.1839	0.1228	0.0826	0.0462
23	0.5067	0.3256	0.1703	0.1117	0.0738	0.0402
24	0.4919	0.3101	0.1577	0.1015	0.0659	0.0349
25	0.4776	0.2953	0.1460	0.0923	0.0588	0.0304
26	0.4637	0.2812	0.1352	0.0839	0.0525	0.0264
27	0.4502	0.2678	0.1252	0.0763	0.0469	0.0230
28	0.4371	0.2551	0.1159	0.0693	0.0419	0.0200
29	0.4243	0.2429	0.1073	0.0630	0.0374	0.0174
30	0.4120	0.2314	0.0994	0.0573	0.0334	0.0151
31	0.4000	0.2204	0.0920	0.0521	0.0298	0.0131
32	0.3883	0.2099	0.0852	0.0474	0.0266	0.0114
33	0.3770	0.1999	0.0789	0.0431	0.0238	0.0099
34	0.3660	0.1904	0.0730	0.0391	0.0212	0.0086
35	0.3554	0.1813	0.0676	0.0356	0.0189	0.0075
40	0.3066	0.1420	0.0460	0.0221	0.0107	0.0037
60	0.1697	0.0535	0.0099	0.0033	0.0011	0.0002
80	0.0940	0.0202	0.0021	0.0005	0.0001	0.0000

Note: t, number of years from present; r, social rate of return.

mums or minimums in each case. Even where potential errors are not quantifiable, it is advisable to think about the direction of their possible influence on the results.

The data demands of the cost-benefit approach are so heavy, particularly on the outcome side, that it is often necessary to look for a shortcut such as the following formula.

$$\frac{B}{C} = \frac{Y_k - Y_{k-\Delta s}}{C}$$

where Y_k is the present value of the mean or median annual earnings of a sample of graduates from the training program at the time of the interview; $Y_{k-\Delta s}$ is the present value of the mean or median of their estimates of what they would have been earning if they had not undergone the particular training program; and C is the present value of the stream of total costs of the program divided by the total number of graduates. Though expressed here as a benefit-cost ratio, this information could be used to calculate net present value or internal rate of return in the usual way.

Labor Market Indicators

Formal cost-outcome analyses are also supplemented by analyzing indicators of the state of the part of the labor market that is relevant to the training program. Ideally, changes in such indicators over the lifetime of the project should be inspected for evidence of impact, but if this is not possible, some inferences about the immediate impact and long-term effects of the project can be drawn from an analysis of current information alone.

Some information can be derived from questionnaires or interviews administered to training institutions and graduates. For instance, what is the employment rate of graduates, say, one year after graduation? Or what proportion of those employed are working in fields similar to those for which they were trained?

More general labor market information—available from such sources as the personnel department of the civil service or of the public sector as a whole, official employment exchanges, private recruitment agencies, and newspaper advertisements—may also be useful for this purpose. An example of relevant data is the number of unfilled vacancies currently being advertised by employers for the occupational category of interest. However, data on vacancies must be treated with care. Vacancies are often filled internally rather than being advertised or reported to employment exchanges. Particularly within the public sector, the number of "vacancies" reported in interviews or questionnaires often represents posts it would be desirable to fill if funds were available, rather than posts for which active recruitment (backed by the power to pay) is in process.

It is a common practice to combine information about vacancies with information about unemployment of people in the same occupational category. Thus if the ratio of unemployed to vacancies is equal to one, this part of the labor market is judged to be in balance; if the ratio is below one (that is, the number of vacancies exceeds the number of unemployed), the employment climate is said to be favorable. However, even in industrialized countries with highly developed social security and employment exchange systems, the ratio of unemployed to vacancies has not been found to be a reliable indicator. In countries where few people register with the official employment exchanges and where many of those who do are not unemployed but are looking for something better, this ratio is likely to be even less helpful.

The number of expatriates employed in the relevant job category may also be a useful indicator of present excess demand. Such information is usually held by the immigration department.

An indicator of the demand for the type of training offered is the number of applications in relation to places; the higher the ratio of applicants to places, the higher the probable payoff to graduates of this type of training.

Finally, the evaluators may look at the impact on earnings over time of the type of training in question. If relative earnings of this occupation vis à vis similar occupations are rising, this may signal an emerging shortage.

The Equity Objective

So far we have implicitly confined ourselves to the efficiency objective of the project. But we have also assumed a concern with equity. How do we incorporate this into our analysis?

Our first task is to establish the private profitability of the training. For this purpose we use the same internal rate of return equation as before, but with costs and benefits defined in private rather than social terms. Thus C is defined as the private cost (the cost to the individual) of the training in question and B as the private benefit (the excess of posttax annual earnings of a person trained at this level over one trained at the level immediately below, net of income forgone during training). If this return is judged to be adequate, we compare the proportion of students from underprivileged groups with a target quota, perhaps based on the proportion of the total population represented by such groups. This is expressed in indicator form as U_t / U_p, where U_t is the proportion of the trainees in this program from the underprivileged group and U_p is the proportion of the total population represented by the underprivileged group. The aim is to achieve as high a value as possible for U_t / U_p, and certainly a value of greater than one. What is possible may be partly determined by cost. For example, abolition of fees or the provision of free meals for underprivileged students may be ways of increasing equity in access (they would also increase private profitability by reducing the private cost to the individual trainee), but the cost to government of such measures may be unacceptably high.

Finally, when a government is seriously engaged in restructuring its strategy toward satisfaction of basic needs and alleviation of poverty, an equity-oriented training policy takes on an extra task: that of imparting the skills required to produce goods and services for the underprivileged. There is no simple indicator of the extent to which a particular training program is oriented toward the needs of the underprivileged rather than the purchasing power of the privileged. The evaluators can begin by determining whether the syllabus of the program (and the job definition from which it derives) is need oriented or market oriented. A basic needs profile of the whole economy, combining data on income distribution and on deficiencies in satisfaction of basic needs, can be useful for this purpose. From such a profile it should be possible to identify types of training that are most relevant to the needs of the poorest. This may not always be easy. For instance, the skills needed to build a public transport vehicle may not be easily distinguishable from those required for sports car manufacture. And the foreign exchange earned by luxury exports may be used to import goods needed for development and for mass consumption. In other cases, however, the distinction will be clear: for instance, training for rural preventive health care as against urban hospital-based curative medicine, or for low-cost housing design as against luxury high-rise buildings.

However, a further check is needed on the effectiveness of need-oriented training. What proportion of graduates from the program actually find jobs doing need-oriented work? Will their need-oriented skills be demanded in the labor market? Broader government strategy and socioeconomic progress are important here if the training program is to have the desired effect.

4

Summary Assessment and Procedures

The main purpose of this manual is to provide management with a diagnostic tool for identifying areas that require improvement. However, it can also be used to provide a profile of an institution so that different institutions within a training system can be compared with each other or with a "standard" institution.

The summary assessment (table 4.1) is meant to facilitate both uses by telescoping the data gathered through questionnaires and observations into a convenient numeric profile. The summary is organized according to indicators of internal and external efficiency. A six-point scale is used, with values ranging from 1 for satisfactory to 6 for unsatisfactory. (For a fuller explanation of the scale, see appendix A.) Since no ranking or weighting of the key factors exists, the summary cannot be made much more compact—it is not possible to arrive at a single measure of the efficiency and effectiveness of a training institution. Instead, the summary provides a multidimensional picture of an institution and permits comparisons between schools.

It should be noted that the overall assessment is not an arithmetic average of all the items under the key factor. The evaluators should weigh the individual responses and make an intuitive judgment of the overall assessment.

The guidelines in this section will be particularly useful for ministries or agencies which have not yet conducted regular evaluations of their technical schools or vocational training centers. We have tried to achieve an appropriate balance of detail and coverage so that the evaluations can be carried out with reasonable expenditures of time and manpower and still provide a systematic and comprehensive evaluation of the performance of any institution. The guidelines are not rules. We expect that in practice they will be modified to suit local circumstances and purposes. The scope of the evaluation and the depth of detail will be decided with an eye to the cost, the staff available, and the use to be made of the results. In the same way, the procedures for conducting the evaluation will vary according to circumstances.

The technical and vocational education system may include tens or hundreds of institutions. If the number is large, we recommend that as a first stage a sample of about ten, representative in terms of type, size, location, and so on, be chosen for initial evaluation. These initial evaluations serve several purposes. They quickly lead to the identification of any common problems or issues. They also allow the guidelines to be adapted and questionnaires and instruments to be modified to suit the agency's needs. If the agency is attempting evaluation on a significantly more detailed basis than in the past, these initial evaluations also provide a training

Table 4.1. *Summary Assessment*

EFFICIENCY OF OPERATIONS

Qualitative Indicators

Content and quality of courses

Format and content of curricula and syllabuses	1 2 3 4 5 6
Quality of curricula and syllabuses	1 2 3 4 5 6
Review and revision of curricula and syllabuses	1 2 3 4 5 6
Teaching methods	1 2 3 4 5 6
Examinations and assessment	1 2 3 4 5 6

Overall assessment: 1 2 3 4 5 6

Students or trainees

Entry and selection 1 2 3 4 5 6
Counseling and career guidance 1 2 3 4 5 6
Staff-student relationships 1 2 3 4 5 6

Overall assessment: 1 2 3 4 5 6

Staffing and staff development

Staffing policies 1 2 3 4 5 6
Selection and qualifications 1 2 3 4 5 6
Staff development and training 1 2 3 4 5 6
Support staff 1 2 3 4 5 6

Overall assessment: 1 2 3 4 5 6

Physical resources

Teaching facilities 1 2 3 4 5 6
Support facilities 1 2 3 4 5 6
Utilization of space 1 2 3 4 5 6
Provision of equipment 1 2 3 4 5 6
Equipment utilization 1 2 3 4 5 6
Consumable materials 1 2 3 4 5 6

Overall assessment: 1 2 3 4 5 6

Organization and management

Objectives and plans 1 2 3 4 5 6
Organizational structure 1 2 3 4 5 6
Information system 1 2 3 4 5 6
Management style and effectiveness 1 2 3 4 5 6

Overall assessment: 1 2 3 4 5 6

Interrelations with industry

Training and employment 1 2 3 4 5 6
Formal links and services 1 2 3 4 5 6
Industrial links of staff 1 2 3 4 5 6
Industrial environment 1 2 3 4 5 6

Overall assessment: 1 2 3 4 5 6

Table 4.1 (*continued*)

Quantitative Indicators

Average time required to produce a graduate ÷ planned
  time   _____
Output-input ratio   _____
Cost per student per year[1]   _____
Cost per graduate   _____
Cost per student ÷ cost per student in general high
  school   _____

EXTERNAL EFFICIENCY (OUTCOMES AND COSTS)[2]

Employers' opinions on employability of graduates
Preferred to other applicants   ☐
Same as other applicants   ☐
Less qualified than other applicants   ☐
No opinion   ☐

Teachers' opinions of graduates
Well prepared for a good job   ☐
Only adequately prepared for a job   ☐
Not well prepared for a job   ☐

Graduates' opinions on their ability to secure
  employment in their field of training
With my training it is easy to get a job   ☐
With my training it is not easy to get a job   ☐
With my training it is very difficult to get a job   ☐

Employment rate of graduates one year after graduation   _____
Proportion of those employed working in the same or
  similar fields for which they were trained   _____
Rate of return of the program (as calculated in chapter 3)   _____

---

1. For short courses use cost per student per hour.
2. Based on interviews with employers, teachers, and graduates, and on quantitative indicators (where data are available) on employment and earnings of graduates.

experience for the staff. The early evaluations should also be designed to help the evaluators arrive at a reasonable consensus of standards through exchange of information and by varying the membership of teams.

If the ministry or agency is establishing regular evaluation as part of its management review process, it is advisable to set up a small unit responsible for the administration of evaluation. However, it is normally better not to create a team of full-time evaluators, but instead to create a panel or pool of senior ministry staff that also includes active principals or directors and, if possible, representatives from industry or technical ministries.

Internal Efficiency

Each institution to be evaluated is given a set of questionnaires to be completed in advance (appendix D), together with a general note prepared by the agency explaining the purpose of the evaluation. If possible, preliminary briefing meetings are held with the directors of the institutions and their senior staff so that the questionnaires can be distributed and the purpose of the evaluation explained. The briefings should stress the importance of evaluation in planning and its value in identifying needs for resources. The full cooperation of staff should be obtained; subsequently, throughout the conduct of the evaluation, the team members must be on their guard to avoid acting as inspectors or inquisitors. Opportunities should be taken to exchange experiences and provide advice as well as to gather information.

The evaluation of the school or center takes place one to four weeks after the questionnaires are distributed. The evaluation team should include at least two persons: a technical and vocational educator whose experience and knowledge cover both developing and developed countries, and a person with a background in economics, particularly manpower and labor market economics. The evaluation of specialized training programs may require the addition of relevant specialists. The team will establish its own work pattern. We suggest the procedure outlined below, using the checklists in appendixes A and B as the main framework and the questionnaires and forms in appendixes D and E to provide the detailed structure for interviews and data collection.

DAY 1. An initial meeting with the principal or director and key senior staff is held. The data, reports, and completed questionnaires that were requested in advance (appendix D) are presented to the team, and problems or missing data are identified (about two hours).

The team then makes a brief tour of the institution to gain familiarity with the main facilities and layout (about one hour).

Next, the team reviews the completed questionnaires and clarifies any apparent anomalies or errors in the answers. It then proceeds, in discussion with the director or principal and the senior staff, to complete appendix questionnaires E.1 through E.7 (about three hours). These questionnaires are to be used as a basis for structured interviews and need not be rigidly followed. To preserve confidentiality, the team may wish to interview the director alone to complete questionnaire E.1, but senior staff should be brought in for the subsequent discussions, both to take advantage of their knowledge and to give them experience in the process of conducting evaluations.

DAY 2. The evaluation team proceeds to the detailed observation of teaching and training activities and use of equipment and facilities. Questionnaires E.8 through E.15 are filled out at this stage. If there is a relatively large number of laboratories or workshops, it is advisable to choose only a sample for detailed study. During this period in the classrooms, laboratories, and workshops the evaluation team should review critically the content and treatment of the courses or subjects (about four hours).

The evaluation team may conduct its interviews of teaching staff and trainees while carrying out the observations in the classrooms and workshops, If, however, only a relatively small sample of the activities is covered, it would be better to arrange for more broadly based interviews with a group of six to eight staff members and a like group of trainees, using questionnaires E.14 and E.15 as the framework (about two hours).

At this stage the evaluation team should be able to complete its assessments of the key factors in checklists A and B, covering the qualitative and quantitative aspects of internal efficiency (about three hours).

A third day may be required if a very large institution (2,000 or more training places and a wide range of training programs) is being evaluated.

The evaluation team concludes its visit to the institution with a brief presentation to the senior staff of the main findings.

It will be clear from the above that the evaluation exercise is significantly more searching and revealing than the normal institutional visit, and only with practice will the team acquire the skills necessary to carry out the interviews and assemble the data. Since the team is required to make value judgments about quality of training, it is vital that the members' experience and background give them adequate status. Even so, they may find it difficult to make judgments about the quality of teaching in subjects that are outside their own specializations. In that case it would be advisable to form slightly larger teams covering a representative range of the technical specializations offered in the institution.

External Efficiency

The evaluation of external efficiency involves the collection of data from employers and graduates of the training programs, as set out in chapter 3. Arrangements for the interviews should be made beforehand, either by the local representatives of the responsible agency or by the director of the institution. It is useful for a staff member of the institution being evaluated (preferably the guidance counselor or the person in charge of liaison with industry) to be present.

THE SAMPLE. Only a sample of firms should be singled out for interviews, that is, six to eight in the city where centers or schools are being evaluated. The firms should be selected on the basis of two criteria: high probability of employing graduates from the institutions being evaluated, and size (large, medium, and small firms should be represented). The information is collected in interviews, initially with the personnel officer, then with foremen and with graduates of the school or recent trainees. These interviews, based on the questionnaires in appendix F, will usually require not more than one to two hours in each firm. The limited purpose of the evaluation should be made clear from the outset, and firms will usually give full cooperation.

THE QUESTIONNAIRE. As discussed in chapter 3, interviews and questionnaires, although costly and time-consuming, are extremely helpful in assessing the effectiveness of the training from the points of view of the trainee and the employer.

In planning a questionnaire survey, the first issue to be resolved is what groups to interview. At a minimum, graduates, dropouts, and supervisors of the graduates should be interviewed. However, if time and resources allow, teachers, directors of programs, and other employers could also be included.

The second issue is what areas to cover. In general, the questionnaires should include the characteristics of the respondent, the effects of training on employment and earnings, assessment of the training program, and assessment of the graduates.

For inquiry through questionnaires to succeed, efficient management and the cooperation of everyone concerned are required. In addition, attention must be given to the following considerations.

Drafting the questions requires great care. It demands a good knowledge of the language and culture of the interviewees, as well as some technical knowledge of the skill or occupation of interest. Whenever possible, questions should not be open-ended, since this invites a wide range of subjective replies and comments that are not comparable. Specific alternative replies to each question should therefore be offered to respondents. This also permits easy coding and tabulation of replies (see sample questionnaires in appendix F).

Better-educated respondents may be able to complete a well-made questionnaire by themselves, and budget limits may necessitate this shortcut. But in general, personal interviewing, although costly, yields the most complete and useful responses, since the interviewer is able to clear up misunderstandings and ask follow-up questions. At the very least, personal delivery and collection of the questionnaires, despite the expense, is preferable to expecting people to reply to an impersonal survey by mail.

Under ideal circumstances a significant statistical sample of former trainees should be drawn. When availability of funds determines the size and structure of the sample and the questionnaire or interview procedure, the only option may be to restrict the interviews to graduates at their place of work. This precludes interviewing unemployed trainees.

Training and instructions for interviewers must be careful and detailed to ensure uniform interpretation of the questions and the smooth evolution of the interview.

Finally the answers have to be coded, tabulated, and cross-tabulated so that the evaluator can draw the pertinent conclusions. Sufficient resources, time, and people must be allocated to do this routine but essential chore properly.

Similar answers to the same question, but from different viewpoints, reinforce conclusions. Conversely, answers that differ from one group to another may cast doubt on the validity of a single conclusion, and further evidence may be required. When graduates of the school are being appraised, a supervisor may be asked to rate graduates compared with nongraduates and a graduate may be asked to rate fellow graduates compared with other workers in his group. Similarly the graduate's assessment of the quality of teachers should be supplemented by the opinions of administrators. Because of the variety of institutional setups and the different characteristics of particular national and cultural environments, it is impossible to spell out beforehand the exact questions to be asked and the manner in which they are posed. But some basic issues are common to all evaluations and must be covered in questionnaires and interviews.

APPENDIXES

Checklist. Efficiency of Operations: Qualitative Evaluation

Note: Refer to completed appendixes D and E.

This checklist covers the key factors to be assessed by the evaluation team. For each key factor there is a set of questions that can be answered easily by checking the appropriate box; space for supplementary comments or explanations; and a block for overall assessment of performance for the key factor. The aim is not to arrive at an overall score based on adding up points for the individual factors. It is to compile a profile of the satisfactory and unsatisfactory aspects of performance for each factor.

The key factors cannot be evaluated without collecting and understanding a considerable amount of data and information and observing the school's operations. Forms and questionnaires for collecting the information and for recording observations are given in appendixes D and E.

Ratings used for the six-point scale are as follows:

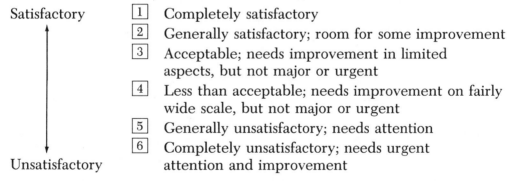

Satisfactory
- 1 Completely satisfactory
- 2 Generally satisfactory; room for some improvement
- 3 Acceptable; needs improvement in limited aspects, but not major or urgent
- 4 Less than acceptable; needs improvement on fairly wide scale, but not major or urgent
- 5 Generally unsatisfactory; needs attention
- 6 Completely unsatisfactory; needs urgent attention and improvement

Unsatisfactory

In general, ratings of 4, 5, and 6 indicate a need for attention and improvement—in the case of 6, an urgent and critical need.

The evaluator should weigh the individual responses and use intuitive judgment to arrive at the overall assessment.

In all checklists, Y stands for yes and N for no.

Content and Quality of Courses

Format and Content of Curricula and Syllabuses

a. How satisfactorily are the course objectives expressed
    and related to training needs?   ☐1 ☐2 ☐3 ☐4 ☐5 ☐6

b. Is there a clear and detailed description of:
    Time allocation for subjects?   ☐Y ☐N
    Time allocation for activities?   ☐Y ☐N
    Subject content?   ☐Y ☐N
    Learning objectives?   ☐Y ☐N
    Performance measures?   ☐Y ☐N

c. How well does the content of curricula and syllabuses
    satisfy course objectives?   ☐1 ☐2 ☐3 ☐4 ☐5 ☐6

d. If the answer to (c) is 4, 5, or 6, indicate the main
    deficiencies:
    Too much theory   ☐
    Does not provide appropriate level of practical
        training   ☐
    Too little theory   ☐
    Curricula content not relevant to industries' needs ☐
    Time allocation not adequate for content   ☐
    Other (list)   ☐

e.   Does the course include project work?   ☐Y ☐N

Comments:

Overall assessment: ☐1 ☐2 ☐3 ☐4 ☐5 ☐6

Quality of Curricula and Syllabuses

a. In relation to the course objectives,
  How well are major practical skills covered? ☐1 ☐2 ☐3 ☐4 ☐5 ☐6
  How well are relevant theoretical areas covered? ☐1 ☐2 ☐3 ☐4 ☐5 ☐6
  How satisfactorily are theoretical and practical
    areas coordinated? ☐1 ☐2 ☐3 ☐4 ☐5 ☐6
b. How satisfactorily are different subjects in the courses
  coordinated? ☐1 ☐2 ☐3 ☐4 ☐5 ☐6
c. How satisfactorily does the overall treatment
  correspond to current and foreseeable industrial
  needs? ☐1 ☐2 ☐3 ☐4 ☐5 ☐6
d. If the responses above include 4, 5, or 6, indicate
  the main deficiencies.

Comments:

Overall assessment: ☐1 ☐2 ☐3 ☐4 ☐5 ☐6

Review and Revision of Curricula and Syllabuses

a. Are curricula and syllabuses reviewed and revised
  regularly? ☐Y ☐N
b. Is industry involved in such reviews? ☐Y ☐N
c. How many years has it been since the last review? ☐<1 ☐1 ☐2 ☐3 ☐>3
d. Is there an arrangement for feedback from graduates
  on course content? ☐Y ☐N

Comments:

Overall assessment: ☐1 ☐2 ☐3 ☐4 ☐5 ☐6

Teaching Methods

a. On the basis of observation, rate—
  The use of teaching and training aids   [1] [2] [3] [4] [5] [6]
  The supply of notes or materials to students   [1] [2] [3] [4] [5] [6]
  The quality of teaching materials   [1] [2] [3] [4] [5] [6]
  The quality of students' work   [1] [2] [3] [4] [5] [6]
b. Taking practical work alone,
  How satisfactory is the quality of students' work?   [1] [2] [3] [4] [5] [6]
  Do the range and quantity of work appear
    satisfactory?   [1] [2] [3] [4] [5] [6]
c. When observed,
  What was the actual size of the practical work
    group?   _____
  Were the trainees being satisfactorily supervised?   [1] [2] [3] [4] [5] [6]
  Approximately what percentage of students in the
    laboratory or workshop actually were performing
    practical work?   _____
d. Does there appear to be satisfactory coordination
  between
  Theory and practice?   [Y] [N]
  Subjects?   [Y] [N]
Comments:

Overall assessment: [1] [2] [3] [4] [5] [6]

Examinations and Assessment

a. Is there a clear description of the examination
  scheme?   [Y] [N]
b. How well does the examination scheme relate to
  course objectives?   [1] [2] [3] [4] [5] [6]
c. How satisfactory are the arrangements for
  determining passing or failure?   [1] [2] [3] [4] [5] [6]
d. How satisfactory are the arrangements for continuous
  assessment?   [1] [2] [3] [4] [5] [6]
Comments:

Overall assessment: [1] [2] [3] [4] [5] [6]

Students and Trainees

Entry and Selection

a. Are entry qualifications satisfactory in relation to course objectives? [Y] [N]

b. Is the selection process appropriate in relation to objectives? [Y] [N]

c. How satisfactory does the quality of students seem in relation to course objectives? [1] [2] [3] [4] [5] [6]

Comments:

Overall assessment: [1] [2] [3] [4] [5] [6]

Counseling and Career Guidance

a. Is there a satisfactory scheme for advising potential students and trainees about courses and careers? [Y] [N]

b. Are there satisfactory arrangements for counseling students on the progress of their training? [Y] [N]

c. Is there a satisfactory scheme for assisting students to find employment? [Y] [N]

d. Is there a formal scheme for follow-up of students after graduation? [Y] [N]

Comments:

Overall assessment: [1] [2] [3] [4] [5] [6]

Staff-Student Relationships

a. Do staff-student relationships appear satisfactory?   [Y] [N]

b. Do students and trainees participate in meetings with staff on training?   [Y] [N]

Comments: (refer also to interviews with staff and students):

Overall assessment: [1] [2] [3] [4] [5] [6]

Staffing and Staff Development

Staffing Policies

a. What is the weekly teaching duty, in hours? _____
b. Are teaching duty hours satisfactory, bearing in mind such factors as the time required for preparation? ☐Y ☐N
c. Are salaries for teachers equivalent to salaries in industry for comparable qualifications? ☐Y ☐N
d. Are other conditions equivalent to those in industry? ☐Y ☐N
e. Is there a satisfactory scheme for grading staff in relation to experience, qualifications, and responsibilities? ☐Y ☐N

Comments:

Overall assessment: ☐1 ☐2 ☐3 ☐4 ☐5 ☐6

Selection and Qualifications

a. In relation to course objectives, are the qualifications and experience required for staff appointment—
    Satisfactory? ☐Y ☐N
    Relevant? ☐Y ☐N
b. How experienced and qualified are the staff with respect to—
    Theoretical training? ☐1 ☐2 ☐3 ☐4 ☐5 ☐6
    Practical skills training? ☐1 ☐2 ☐3 ☐4 ☐5 ☐6
    Training in teaching? ☐1 ☐2 ☐3 ☐4 ☐5 ☐6
    Industrial experience? ☐1 ☐2 ☐3 ☐4 ☐5 ☐6
c. Are the conditions for promotion satisfactory? ☐Y ☐N
d. Is there a satisfactory number of staff in post? ☐Y ☐N
e. Is the turnover reasonable? ☐Y ☐N

Comments:

Overall assessment: ☐1 ☐2 ☐3 ☐4 ☐5 ☐6

Staff Development and Training

a. Is there a satisfactory staff development plan for the institution?   [Y] [N]

b. Are there satisfactory arrangements for pre-service training in—
    Technical competence?   [Y] [N]
    Teaching methods?   [Y] [N]
    Management?   [Y] [N]

c. Are there satisfactory arrangements for in-service training?   [Y] [N]

Comments:

Overall assessment: [1] [2] [3] [4] [5] [6]

Support Staff

a. Are the following staff levels satisfactory?
    Technical support staff for laboratories and
      workshops   [Y] [N]
    Administrative staff   [Y] [N]
    Specialist staff, for example, librarians   [Y] [N]
    Storekeepers   [Y] [N]

b. Are there satisfactory numbers of staff actually in the following posts?
    Technical support staff for laboratories and
      workshops   [Y] [N]
    Administrative staff   [Y] [N]
    Specialist staff, for example, librarians   [Y] [N]
    Storekeepers   [Y] [N]

c. Are salary levels for support personnel adequate to attract staff?   [Y] [N]

d. How qualified and experienced are the support staff?   [1] [2] [3] [4] [5] [6]

Comments:

Overall assessment: [1] [2] [3] [4] [5] [6]

Physical Resources

Teaching Facilities

a. Are the amounts and range of the following
   satisfactory?
      Classrooms   [Y] [N]
      Specialist laboratories   [Y] [N]
      Specialist workshops   [Y] [N]
      Preparation rooms and stores   [Y] [N]

b. Is the physical layout and interrelationship
   satisfactory?   [Y] [N]

c. Are services adequate?   [Y] [N]

d. Are buildings and services maintained in a
   satisfactory state?   [Y] [N]

e. Are safety features satisfactory?   [Y] [N]

f. Are lighting and ventilation satisfactory?   [Y] [N]

Comments:

Overall assessment: [1] [2] [3] [4] [5] [6]

Support Facilities

a. Are the areas and facilities for the following
   satisfactory?
      Library   [Y] [N]
      Administration   [Y] [N]
      Central services   [Y] [N]
      Communal areas   [Y] [N]

b. Is student housing adequate?   [Y] [N]

c. Is staff housing adequate?   [Y] [N]

Comments:

Overall assessment: 

Utilization of Space (see appendix B, "Facilities: Schedule and Utilization")

a. How satisfactory is the utilization of the following?

Classrooms	① ② ③ ④ ⑤ ⑥
Laboratories	① ② ③ ④ ⑤ ⑥
Workshops	① ② ③ ④ ⑤ ⑥
Libraries	① ② ③ ④ ⑤ ⑥
Other	① ② ③ ④ ⑤ ⑥

Comments:

Overall assessment: ① ② ③ ④ ⑤ ⑥

Provision of Equipment

a. How comprehensive is the range of laboratory and workshop equipment?   ① ② ③ ④ ⑤ ⑥

b. How relevant is the equipment to course needs?   ① ② ③ ④ ⑤ ⑥

c. How satisfactory is the provision of equipment for individual practical work?   ① ② ③ ④ ⑤ ⑥

d. How satisfactory is the equipment in terms of being up to date?   ① ② ③ ④ ⑤ ⑥

e. How adequate is the provision and availability of the following support equipment?

Overhead projectors	① ② ③ ④ ⑤ ⑥
Screens	① ② ③ ④ ⑤ ⑥
Reprographic equipment	① ② ③ ④ ⑤ ⑥
Other audiovisual aids	① ② ③ ④ ⑤ ⑥

f. How satisfactory is the program for replacement of equipment?   ① ② ③ ④ ⑤ ⑥

Comments:

Overall assessment: ① ② ③ ④ ⑤ ⑥

Equipment Utilization

a. How satisfactory is the utilization of equipment? ☐1 ☐2 ☐3 ☐4 ☐5 ☐6
b. What are the main reasons for equipment not being
   in regular use?
    Lack of materials ☐Y ☐N
    Not relevant to course needs ☐Y ☐N
    Obsolete ☐Y ☐N
    No instruction manuals ☐Y ☐N
    Broken down; lack of spares ☐Y ☐N
c. How satisfactory is the maintenance program? ☐1 ☐2 ☐3 ☐4 ☐5 ☐6
d. How satisfactory is the stock of spare parts? ☐1 ☐2 ☐3 ☐4 ☐5 ☐6

Comments:

Overall assessment: ☐1 ☐2 ☐3 ☐4 ☐5 ☐6

Consumable Materials

a. How satisfactory are stocks of consumable materials? ☐1 ☐2 ☐3 ☐4 ☐5 ☐6
b. How satisfactory is the stores and distribution system? ☐1 ☐2 ☐3 ☐4 ☐5 ☐6
c. Are there satisfactory provisions in annual budgets
   for replacing materials? ☐Y ☐N
d. How satisfactory are the availability of materials and
   their use in the training? ☐1 ☐2 ☐3 ☐4 ☐5 ☐6

Comments:

Overall assessment: ☐1 ☐2 ☐3 ☐4 ☐5 ☐6

Organization and Management

Objectives and Plans

a. How clearly are institutional objectives defined?   ⬚1 ⬚2 ⬚3 ⬚4 ⬚5 ⬚6

b. To what extent is there an institutional development
plan covering
    Course development?   ⬚1 ⬚2 ⬚3 ⬚4 ⬚5 ⬚6
    Enrollments?   ⬚1 ⬚2 ⬚3 ⬚4 ⬚5 ⬚6
    Staffing?   ⬚1 ⬚2 ⬚3 ⬚4 ⬚5 ⬚6
    Physical resources?   ⬚1 ⬚2 ⬚3 ⬚4 ⬚5 ⬚6
    Capital and recurrent costs?   ⬚1 ⬚2 ⬚3 ⬚4 ⬚5 ⬚6

c. Are plans reviewed regularly and implementation
monitored?   ⬚Y ⬚N

d. How effective is the system for monitoring
implementation of development plans?   ⬚1 ⬚2 ⬚3 ⬚4 ⬚5 ⬚6

Comments:

Overall assessment: ⬚1 ⬚2 ⬚3 ⬚4 ⬚5 ⬚6

Organizational Structure

a. How clear and well defined is the organizational
structure?   ⬚1 ⬚2 ⬚3 ⬚4 ⬚5 ⬚6

b. Does the structure match the training functions?   ⬚1 ⬚2 ⬚3 ⬚4 ⬚5 ⬚6

c. Is there a local governing body?   ⬚Y ⬚N

d. If yes, is industry represented?   ⬚Y ⬚N

Comments:

Overall assessment: ⬚1 ⬚2 ⬚3 ⬚4 ⬚5 ⬚6

Information System

a. How adequate and readily available is information
   on

    Enrollments?   ☐1 ☐2 ☐3 ☐4 ☐5 ☐6

    Student and trainee performance?   ☐1 ☐2 ☐3 ☐4 ☐5 ☐6

    Utilization of resources?   ☐1 ☐2 ☐3 ☐4 ☐5 ☐6

    Expenditure and income?   ☐1 ☐2 ☐3 ☐4 ☐5 ☐6

b. Is such information used in decisionmaking?   ☐Y ☐N

Comments:

Overall assessment: ☐1 ☐2 ☐3 ☐4 ☐5 ☐6

Management Style and Effectiveness

a. How well do the staff exhibit a sense of purpose and
   understanding of objectives?   ☐1 ☐2 ☐3 ☐4 ☐5 ☐6

b. How well do students and trainees exhibit a sense
   of purpose and understanding of objectives?   ☐1 ☐2 ☐3 ☐4 ☐5 ☐6

c. What is the state of discipline in the institution?   ☐1 ☐2 ☐3 ☐4 ☐5 ☐6

d. Overall, how well managed does the institution
   appear to be?   ☐1 ☐2 ☐3 ☐4 ☐5 ☐6

Comments:

Overall assessment: ☐1 ☐2 ☐3 ☐4 ☐5 ☐6

Interrelations with Industry

Training and Employment

a. Approximately what percentage of trainees obtains jobs in their fields within six months after finishing training?

<5 ☐ 6–20 ☐ 21–40 ☐ 41–60 ☐ 61–80 ☐ >80 ☐

b. What percentage of trainees on full-time or block-release programs is sponsored by industry?

<5 ☐ 6–20 ☐ 21–40 ☐ 41–60 ☐ 61–80 ☐ >80 ☐

c. Does industry have employees who have had in-plant training take skills tests conducted by the institution?   Y N

d. How effective is the organization or service provided by the institution to help trainees obtain employment after they finish training?   1 2 3 4 5 6

   Is there a full-time placement officer?   Y N

   Is there a part-time placement officer?   Y N

   Does industry regularly visit the institution to recruit workers?   Y N

e. How effective is the institution's follow-up of trainees to obtain feedback information on training and employment?   1 2 3 4 5 6

Comments:

Overall assessment: 1 2 3 4 5 6

Formal Links and Services

a. How effective is the participation of industry
   representatives in the following activities?
   - Governing body of the institution `1` `2` `3` `4` `5` `6`
   - Advisory committee `1` `2` `3` `4` `5` `6`
   - Training programs and curricula `1` `2` `3` `4` `5` `6`
   - Examinations or tests `1` `2` `3` `4` `5` `6`
b. Does industry participate in joint publicity or similar
   supporting activities, for example, the award of prizes
   to trainees? `Y` `N`
c. How effectively does the institution provide the
   following services to industry?
   - Technical advice `1` `2` `3` `4` `5` `6`
   - Technical services (measurements, testing) `1` `2` `3` `4` `5` `6`
   - Production assistance `1` `2` `3` `4` `5` `6`

Comments:

Overall assessment: `1` `2` `3` `4` `5` `6`

Industrial Links of Staff

a. How satisfactory is the extent and relevance of the
   teaching staff's experience in industry? `1` `2` `3` `4` `5` `6`
b. Is there a regular arrangement for staff to be attached
   to industry for experience? `Y` `N`
c. Does the institution make effective use of part-time
   staff from industry? `Y` `N`
d. Are there staff members who are responsible for
   liaison with industry? `Y` `N`
e. Do staff obtain any significant income from industry? `Y` `N`

Comments:

Overall assessment: `1` `2` `3` `4` `5` `6`

Industrial Environment

a. How effective is the institution in creating an environment similar to that in industry with respect to

General work environment? ☐1 ☐2 ☐3 ☐4 ☐5 ☐6

Discipline? ☐1 ☐2 ☐3 ☐4 ☐5 ☐6

Timekeeping? ☐1 ☐2 ☐3 ☐4 ☐5 ☐6

Safety procedures? ☐1 ☐2 ☐3 ☐4 ☐5 ☐6

b. Does the institution engage in production, construction, or repair activities? ☐Y ☐N

c. If yes,

Are students effectively involved? ☐Y ☐N

Are staff effectively involved? ☐Y ☐N

How effectively does the activity contribute to the content and standard of training? ☐1 ☐2 ☐3 ☐4 ☐5 ☐6

How effectively does the activity contribute to income generation for the center? ☐1 ☐2 ☐3 ☐4 ☐5 ☐6

Comments:

Overall assessment: ☐1 ☐2 ☐3 ☐4 ☐5 ☐6

Checklist. Efficiency of Operations: Quantitative Evaluation

Note: Refer to completed appendixes D and E.

Student Flow Rates

a. Admission rate   _____
b. Dropout rate   _____
c. Repetition rate   _____
d. Pass/fail rate   _____

Efficiency Indexes

a. Average time required to produce a graduate   _____
b. Output-input ratio   _____

Staff Load

a. Student-staff ratio   _____
b. Average class size   _____
c. Average teacher workload (hours a week)   _____

Facilities: Schedules and Utilization

a. Average workspace per student (in square meters)
     Classrooms   _____
     Laboratories   _____
     Workshops   _____
b. Support space (capacity in square meters per student)
     Library   _____
     Communal space   _____
     Living accommodations   _____
c. Space utilization (list for selected categories of space
        and for specialized workshops and laboratories,
        for example, machine shop, welding workshop)

Costs

a. Total and unit costs
    Total cost   _____
    Number of students   _____
    Number of graduates   _____
    Cost per student per year   _____
    Cost per graduate   _____
b. Cost analysis (show each category as percentage of
    total costs)
    Staff salaries   _____
    Consumable materials   _____
    Maintenance   _____
    Other (break down if exceeds 10 percent)   _____

C

Checklist. The Central Training System

Policies, Planning, and Development

a. Is there a central policy for vocational training and
   education?   ☐Y ☐N
b. Is there satisfactory coordination between the various
   training subsystems?   ☐Y ☐N
c. Is there a current national development plan for
   training?   ☐Y ☐N
d. If yes does the plan adequately cover:
   Enrollments?   ☐Y ☐N
   Training programs?   ☐Y ☐N
   Staffing?   ☐Y ☐N
   Physical resources?   ☐Y ☐N
   Capital costs?   ☐Y ☐N
   Recurrent costs?   ☐Y ☐N

Comments:

Overall assessment: ☐1 ☐2 ☐3 ☐4 ☐5 ☐6

Central and Regional Control

Control of Training Programs and Courses

a. Is the distribution of courses and enrollments
   centrally controlled?   ☐Y ☐N
b. Is there a national training system?   ☐Y ☐N
c. If yes, what percentage of trainees takes national
   standardized tests?   ☐Y ☐N
d. Is there central control of
   Curricula and syllabuses?   ☐Y ☐N
   Content of training materials?   ☐Y ☐N
   Supply of training materials?   ☐Y ☐N
   Examinations?   ☐Y ☐N
e. Is there a system of national inspectors or advisers?   ☐Y ☐N
f. Is quality of training monitored by central staff?   ☐Y ☐N

Comments

Overall assessment: ☐1 ☐2 ☐3 ☐4 ☐5 ☐6

Control of Staffing

a. Are staff salaries fixed nationally?   ☐Y ☐N
b. Are staff levels fixed nationally?   ☐Y ☐N
c. Are salaries comparable with those for other
   government work?   ☐Y ☐N
d. Are salaries comparable with those in the private
   sector?   ☐Y ☐N
e. Is there a national staff development and training
   plan?   ☐Y ☐N
f. Is there adequate provision for the following types
   of in-service training?   ☐Y ☐N
   Technical training   ☐Y ☐N
   Teacher training   ☐Y ☐N
   Management training   ☐Y ☐N
g. Is staff performance monitored?   ☐Y ☐N

Comments:

Overall assessment: ☐1 ☐2 ☐3 ☐4 ☐5 ☐6

Physical Resources

a. Is there a national building development plan that
    is related to academic and training plans?   ☐Y ☐N

b. Are building plans based on standard unit areas per
    trainee place?   ☐Y ☐N

c. If yes, are the standards comparable to international
    standards?   ☐Y ☐N

d. Is utilization of buildings monitored?   ☐Y ☐N

e. Have standards been established for provision of
    Equipment?   ☐Y ☐N
    Materials?   ☐Y ☐N

f. Is equipment utilization monitored?   ☐Y ☐N

Comments:

Overall assessment: ☐1 ☐2 ☐3 ☐4 ☐5 ☐6

Finances

a. What are the sources of funds?
    Government (if so, check appropriate boxes below)   ☐
        Direct budget allocation   ☐
        Earmarked taxes   ☐
        Combination of these two   ☐
    Industry   ☐
    Fees   ☐

b. Are medium or long-term forecasts of availability of
    funds made?   ☐Y ☐N

c. Are costs analyzed?   ☐Y ☐N

d. Are costs and financial data used for management
    purposes?   ☐Y ☐N

Comments:

Overall assessment: ☐1 ☐2 ☐3 ☐4 ☐5 ☐6

Management Organization

a. Does the management organization provide for systematic and effective coverage of responsibilities for

    Planning?   Y   N

    Implementation?   Y   N

    Follow-up?   Y   N

b. Does the management staff appear adequate with respect to

    Numbers?   Y   N

    Training qualifications and experience?   Y   N

    Management qualifications, and experience?   Y   N

c. Is up-to-date information available on

    Enrollments?   Y   N

    Staffing?   Y   N

    Examination results?   Y   N

    Costs?   Y   N

d. Is the information listed in (c) used for management purposes?   Y   N

Comments:

Overall assessment: 1   2   3   4   5   6

Background Information and Questionnaires

Copies of the reports, documents, and statements listed below should be obtained before the evaluation.

- Organization charts of the central ministry and regional office showing relevant key posts and main responsibilities
- Copies or extracts of relevant government policy statements, decrees, development programs, and annual reports
- Regulations covering apprenticeship, training incentives, and so forth.

The following questionnaires should be completed.

- C.1. Annual Enrollments and Output, Technical and Vocational Education and Training Systems
- C.2. Central Agency Expenditures, by Program
- C.3. Sources and Uses of Funds for Training
- C.4. Training Services of the Central Agency

C.1. *Annual Enrollments and Output, Vocational Training System*
Instructions: Complete for past three years.

System	19_/_			19_/_			19_/_		
	Number of schools or centers	Enroll-ment	Output	Number of schools or centers	Enroll-ment	Output	Number of schools or centers	Enroll-ment	Output
Secondary vocational and technical schools									
Public (government)									
Industrial and technical									
Other vocational									
Private									
Industrial and technical									
Other vocational									
Vocational training									
Public (government)									
Industrial vocational training centers									
Other vocational training centers									
Privately financed or industry-sponsored									
Industrial vocational training									
Other vocational training									

C.2. *Central Agency Expenditures, by Program*

Instructions: Record expenditures, in local currency, for each category for the past two years. Separate tables are to be completed for each central agency (ministry of education, ministry of labor or manpower, central training authority).

	19__/__	19__/__
General administration		
Manpower planning		
Training services		
Curriculum development		
Production of teaching materials		
Skills testing		
Inspection		
Advisory services		
Staff development		
Research		
Employment services		
Placement		
Follow-up		
Total		

C.3. *Sources and Uses of Funds for Training*

A. Expenditures on vocational and technical training

Instructions: Give expenditures, in local currency, for past two years.

	19__/__	19__/__
Ministry of education		
a. Total expenditure on vocational and technical education[1]		
b. Expenditure on industrial vocational education[2]		
Ministry of labor or manpower, or central training agency		
a. Total expenditure on vocational training[1]		
b. Expenditure on industrial vocational training[2]		

B. Sources of funds

Instructions: Give data in local currency.

	Regular budget	*Earmarked taxes or levy*	*Income from fees*	*Development funds*	*Other*
Ministry of education					
Ministry of labor or manpower, or central training agency					

1. Includes industrial, agricultural, and home economics.
2. Included in (a).

C.4. Training Services of the Central Agency

Evaluation team: Write in year (most recent full fiscal year).
Instructions: Please provide figures or check appropriate box.

1. Is there a national training advisory service that assists employers to identify training needs and to arrange training? _____

2. If yes,
    a. How many training officers are there? _____
    b. How many firms were assisted in 198_? _____
    c. How many workers were upgraded in 198_? _____
        Of these, how many were
            Apprentices (craft, technical, and engineering)? _____
            Adult workers? _____
            Supervisors and foremen? _____
    d. How much money, in local currency, was budgeted by the government for the service in 198_? _____
    e. How much money, in local currency, did employers contribute to the service in 198_? _____

3. Is training arranged for training officers and managers of firms?   [Y] [N]

4. If yes,
    a. How many training officers and managers were trained in 198_? _____
    b. Were the courses for training officers and managers given by staff of the central training office?   [Y] [N]
    c. If no, were the courses subcontracted to a management training unit of an institution for higher education?   [Y] [N]
    d. How much money, in local currency, was budgeted for this service in 198_? _____

5. Is there an inspection service to supervise training centers and staff?   [Y] [N]

6. If yes,
    a. How many supervisors are employed?   _____
    b. How many training centers were inspected in
       198_?   _____
    c. How long does an inspection normally take?   _____
    b. Does the inspection include
        A review of the course program and lesson
           plans?   Y N
        An assessment of the training methods em-
           ployed?   Y N
        An inspection of the training equipment, materi-
           als, and aids in use?   Y N
        A review of text schemes and the quality of train-
           ees' work?   Y N
        An assessment of the upkeep of workshops and
           offices?   Y N
        An evaluation of the quality of instruction and
           of training center management?   Y N
        A meeting with the advisory body or other group
           of employers regarding the relevance to local
           needs of the training center and its programs?   Y N
        A review of the budget and accounting system?   Y N
    e. Are inspection reports available?   Y N
        If yes, please provide evaluation team with ex-
           amples.
    f. How much money is budgeted for inspection?   _____
7. Are there arrangements for evaluating the external
   efficiency of training programs?   Y N
8. If yes,
    a. Is there a tracer and follow-up system for former
       trainees?   Y N
    b. If yes,
        For how many years after graduation are train-
           ees followed up?   _____
        What is the frequency of follow-up?   _____
        What is the annual budget for follow-up?   _____
    c. Are employers interviewed to ascertain their opin-
       ion of former trainees' performance?   Y N
    d. If yes, are employers questioned on
        Skill levels of former trainees?   Y N
        Relevance of the training?   Y N
        Attitudes of former trainees?   Y N

Efficiency of Operations: Background Information

The information requested in this appendix is to be collected in advance by the director and senior staff of the institution to be evaluated. If the evaluation team is multinational and translations will be needed, ask the responsible person to provide translations or translated summaries of the information, and specify the languages.

The responsible person should place a check mark in each box in the list below to show that the requested information has been gathered or the questionnaires completed. The questionnaires are intended as guides and may be modified by the team to fit the particular circumstances.

1. Basic information (D.1) ☐
2. Course curricula, syllabuses, and examinations
   a. Curricula of main courses showing time allocations by subject for each year or semester ☐
   b. Specimen syllabuses (provide examples for typical courses to show the format) ☐
   c. Examination regulations ☐
3. Students
   a. Entrance qualifications ☐
   b. Enrollment and output, by course (D.2) ☐
   c. Recent report on follow-up of graduates, if available ☐
4. Staff
   a. Curriculum vitae of director ☐
   b. Instructors' qualifications and experience (D.3) ☐
   c. Support staff (D.4) ☐
5. Physical resources
   a. Schedule for facilities (D.5) ☐
   b. Utilization of space (D.6) ☐

6. Management
   a. The institution's organization chart, showing main departments and units, key posts such as heads of departments, and advisory committees. Include brief details of constitution and terms of reference for staff.   ☐
   b. The latest annual report of the institution   ☐
   c. The development plan, if any, for the institution   ☐
7. Costs
   a. Annual operating costs (D.7)   ☐
   b. Capital expenditure (D.8)   ☐

D.1. Basic Information

Name of center or school _____
Address _____
Name of director or head teacher _____
Date institution began operations _____
Main courses or specializations (include brief statement of main training activities):

Total number of students enrolled   _____
Total number of teaching or training staff   _____
Total number of other staff   _____
Does the center or school operate on a single or a double
   shift?   _____
Approximately what percentage of total training hours
   is alloted to
  Regular technical school courses   _____
  Courses for unemployed youth no longer in school   _____
  Courses for apprentices   _____
  Courses to upgrade employed workers   _____
  Supervisory training   _____
  Management training   _____
  Instructor training   _____
  Other   _____

Name and position of person completing questionnaire _____
_____
Date _____

Name of school or center _____

D.2. *Enrollment and Output, by Course or Specialization, 19__/__*

Instructions: Complete a separate table for each of the past three years. This form is suitable for courses lasting one to four years. If courses are shorter than one year, use only the first column. See specific notes below.

Course or specialization[1]	Nature or length of course[2]	First year	Second year	Third year	Fourth year	Total	Output (number of graduates)[3]

All courses

1. List specializations or courses in which training is offered and students are enrolled (for example, mechanical engineering, auto mechanics, welding, electrical installation).

2. Enter separately for each major program or course. Indicate length in weeks or total hours per course or year; show whether course is full time or part time.

3. Number who completed course successfully.

Name of school or center _____

D.3. Instructors' Qualifications and Experience

| Specialization[2] | Number of instructors | | | | Average value for each specialization or trade[1] | | | | | | | |
| | Part-time | | Full-time | Total FTE | Years of general education | Years of technical education or vocational training | Years of technical teacher training | Years of teaching experience | Length of training overseas | Upgrading in-service training | Years of industrial experience | Relative salary[4] |
	Number	FTE[3]										

1. Show the average value for each full-time equivalent (FTE) instructor for each specialization.
2. List specializations according to the main departmental or unit groupings, for example, mechanical, automotive, electrical, building construction, general science, and mathematics.
3. The number of full-time-equivalent teachers is obtained by dividing the total weekly hours (periods) taught by part-time teachers by the normal weekly teaching load of a full-time teacher.
4. Average salary divided by salary of industrial worker with equivalent qualifications.

Name of school or center _____

D.4. *Support Staff*
Instructions: Complete for each of the past three years.

	Number of support staff		
	19__/__	*19__/__*	*19__/__*
Laboratory technicians			
Workshop support staff			
Storekeepers			
Administrative staff			
Specialized support staff (librarians, accountants, and others)			
Total			

Name of school or center _____

D.5. *Schedule for Facilities, 19__/__*
Instructions: Use information for past year.

Purpose	Unit area (approx., in square meters) (1)	Number of units (2)	Capacity (trainee places)	
			Per unit (3)	Total (4)
Teaching				
Classroom[1]				
Laboratories[2]				
Workshops[2]				
Support				
Library				
Audio-visual				
Storage				
Administrative				
Other				
Catering (dining and kitchen)				
Student services				
Residential				
Staff residences (approximate size category and number in that category)				
Total number				
Student dormitories or hostels (total number of places) Male Female				

1. Group classrooms by approximate size.
2. List and group by specialization (include associated preparation rooms).

Name of school or center _____

D.6. *Space Utilization*

Instructions: Provide information for each column (see also example that follows this form).

Col. 1. List spaces by type of use or specialization; for example, classrooms (could be treated as group), drawing offices, laboratories (by specialization, as electrical engineering, mechanical engineering, physics), workshops (by specialization, as mechanical, bench, machine, electrical).

Col. 2. Enter number of workplaces for each group of specialized spaces (from D.5, col. 4).

Col. 3. For the theoretical, or maximum, capacity, multiply the number of workplaces by the hours (or periods) per week that the center or school is open and multiply the product by the number of weeks per year (or semester) that the center or school is open.

Col. 4. For each group of specialized spaces list by year the courses that actually use that facility.

Col. 5. Enter the actual number of students enrolled in the course for the year (or semester).

Col. 6. Enter the hours (or periods) per week when students are actually scheduled to be using the facility (from the course curriculum).

Col. 7. Enter the number of weeks per year (or per semester) when the course actually uses the facility.

Col. 8. Multiply (5) by (6) by (7).

Col. 9. Divide (8) by (3).

Teaching space(s) (1)	Number of workplaces (2)	Capacity in place-hours (or periods) per year (or semester) (3)	Course(s) using the facility (4)	Number of students enrolled in each course (5)	Hours (periods) per week spent in the facility (6)	Number of weeks per year (or semester) for which course uses facility (7)	Actual use in student-hours (or periods) per year (or semester) (8)	Utilization factor (9)

This example illustrates the method for calculating utilization of a mechanical workshop and a physics laboratory where these facilities are used by two courses, a mechanical course and an electrical course.

Teaching space (1)	Courses using facility (4)		Number of students enrolled (5)	Hours or periods per week spent in facility[1] (6)	Number of weeks per year facility used (7)	Actual use in student-hours per year [(7)·(6)·(5)] (8)
Mechanical workshop	Mechanical	First year	50	6	36	10,800
		Second year	40	8	36	11,520
		Third year	38	12	36	16,416
	Electrical	First year	25	2	36	1,800
		Second year	23	2	36	1,656
	Total					42,192
Physics laboratory	Mechanical	First year	50	4	36	7,800
		Second year	40	4	36	5,760
		Third year	38	4	36	5,472
	Electrical	First year	25	4	36	3,600
		Second year	23	4	36	3,312
		Third year	26	4	36	3,744
	Total					29,088

Notes: Column numbers correspond to numbers in D.6. For this example we assume a course length of 36 weeks per year.
1. This information is derived from the school curricula, as shown below (numbers in italics correspond to column 6 in the example).

Curriculum	Mechanical course (hours per week)			Electrical course (hours per week)		
	First year	Second year	Third year	First year	Second year	Third year
Mathematics	6	6	6	6	6	6
Social studies	4	3	2	4	3	2
Physics						
Lab	4	4	4	4	4	4
Theory	2	2	2	2	2	2
Chemistry						
Lab	4	3	2	4	3	2
Theory	2	2	1	2	2	1

Curriculum	Mechanical course (hours per week)			Electrical course (hours per week)		
	First year	Second year	Third year	First year	Second year	Third year
Mechanical						
Workshop	6	8	12	2	2	0
Theory	4	4	6	1	1	0
Electrical						
Workshop	2	2	0	6	8	12
Theory	1	1	0	4	4	6
Total	35	35	35	35	35	35

Name of school or center _____

D.7. *Annual Operating Costs*

Instructions: Complete for each of the past three years. Give expenditures in local currency. Operating costs are actual outlays of funds, regardless of their source. For example, if the government pays some part of salaries and a donor agency others, the combined cost to the government and the agency is recorded.

	Actual expenditure		
Item	*19__/__*	*19__/__*	*19__/__*
Salaries and allowances			
Teachers and instructors			
Salaries			
Other allowances			
Support staff, salaries and allowances			
Consumable materials[1]			
Maintenance of buildings and equipment			
Interest			
Utilities			
Travel			
Boarding costs			
Other[2]			
Total			

1. Consumable materials include such items as metal, wood, building materials, welding rods, oil, paper, small tools, and electronic components. It does not include equipment expected to have a working life of more than two years (for example, lathes, typewriters, and signal generators); these are capital items (see D.8).

2. If more than 10 percent of total expenditure, itemize. This category includes the cost of any student stipends.

D.8. *Capital Expenditure*

Instructions: Complete for each of the past three years. Give expenditures in local currency.

Item or category	*19__/__*	*19__/__*	*19__/__*
Construction			
New equipment and machinery			
Other			
Total			

Efficiency of Operations: Forms for Interviews and Observation

The questionnaires and forms in this appendix are to be completed by the evaluation team. The forms provided here are intended as a guide for systematic collection of information; supplementary questions may be needed to clarify the arrangements in the particular center.

The first step is an initial interview with the director or head teacher, at which questionnaire E.1 is completed.

Next, at a meeting with the director or head teacher and the senior staff, the evaluation team completes a set of questionnaires:

E.2 (Selection and Admission of Students and Trainees)
E.3 (Job Placement and Follow-up)
E.4 (Staff Selection and Promotion)
E.5 (Staff Development Plans)
E.6 (External and Industrial Activities)
E.7 (Management)

The team then observes in detail the institution's teaching and training activities and the use of equipment and facilities. On the basis of these observations and discussions with trainees and staff, the team completes the following forms:

E.8 (Teaching Activities Observed)
E.9 (Quality of Teaching Materials and of Training Programs)
E.10 (Upkeep of Laboratories and Workshops)
E.11 (Utilization of Equipment)
E.12 (Availability and Use of Small Tools and Measuring Equipment)
E.13 Availability and Use of Consumable Materials

The team also completes, in small group (six to eight persons) discussions, E.14 (for instructors) and E.15 (for students).

Name of school or center _____

E.1. Questionnaire for Director or Head Teacher

Instructions: Circle the appropriate answer.

Recruitment and Employment of Teachers and Instructors

1. In your opinion, is it possible to recruit an adequate number of qualified and experienced vocational instructors?
   a. Yes
   b. No
2. If no, why?
   a. Pay is too low to attract experienced people.
   b. This locality is not attractive.
   c. Other (explain)
3. What is the annual turnover of instructors, as a percentage of total teaching staff?
   a. More than 20 percent
   b. 11–19 percent
   c. 5–10 percent
   d. Less than 5 percent
4. If the turnover is greater than 10 percent a year, what is the principal reason?
   a. Death, retirement, or illness
   b. Transfer to private industry
   c. Transfer to other jobs in government service
   d. Transfer to another training center or school
   e. Other (explain)
5. If your staff members are moving to industry or other jobs, what is the reason?
   a. Better pay
   b. Better conditions and benefits
   c. Other (explain)
6. In your judgment, how satisfactory is the performance of your instructors?
   a. Staff as a whole is in need of major training and upgrading.
   b. Most staff need some additional training, skills, and experience.
   c. Generally satisfactory, but some staff members need more training in specific areas.
   d. Satisfactory
7. If staff need more training or experience, in what areas?
   a. Professional or technical knowledge
   b. Practical or technical skills
   c. Ability to teach
   d. Experience in industry
   e. Management training
   f. Other (explain)

Quality of Output and Graduates

8. Are graduates from your program prepared satisfactorily for employment in industry in fields relevant to their training?
    a. Yes
    b. No
9. If no, why?
    a. Training programs are too short.
    b. Teachers are not sufficiently well trained or experienced.
    c. Students are not sufficiently motivated.
    d. Content or balance of training course is not relevant to employment needs.
    e. Facilities and equipment are below standard.
    f. Other (explain)
10. How do your graduates get jobs?
    a. Industry approaches the center or school.
    b. The center or school contacts industries.
    c. Personal initiative is taken by graduates.
    d. Other (explain)
    e. Don't know
11. What percentage of your graduates get jobs in the fields they were trained for?
    a. 76–100 percent
    b. 50–75 percent
    c. Less than 50 percent

General

12. In your opinion, which *two* of the following measures would most improve the training offered in your institution?
    a. Improve buildings
    b. Improve equipment
    c. Change the course of study
    d. Improve training materials
    e. Increase number of instructors
    f. Upgrade instructors
    g. Increase supply of such materials as metals, paper, and spare parts
    h. Improve supervision of the institution by central ministry
    i. Improve guidance and counseling of students
    j. Improve the selection process for incoming students
    k. Establish closer relations with employers and industry
    l. Other (explain)

Name of school or center _____

E.2. Selection and Admission of Students and Trainees

Instructions: For the most recent year, check if applicable or provide information.

1. Total number of applicants   _____
2. Total number of admissions   _____
3. What are the criteria for admission to a course as a
   trainee?
   a. Age (specify)   _____
   b. Years of general education completed (specify)   _____
   c. Nomination by government department   ☐
   d. Sponsorship by industry   ☐
   e. Ability to pay fee   ☐
   f. Not employed   ☐
   g. Other (specify) _____
4. What is the method of selection?
   a. Written information   ☐
   b. Interviews   ☐
   c. Practical test   ☐
   d. Theory test   ☐
   e. Health examination   ☐
   f. Other (specify) _____
5. Is there a special budget for expenditures on selection?   Y N
6. Is there special provision for admission of handi-
   capped trainees?   Y N
7. If yes, give details. _____
8. What percentage of students selected is sponsored
   by
   a. Government departments?   _____
   b. Private industry?   _____
9. What percentage of students admitted is recruited
   from
   a. The town or city in which the center is located? _____
   b. The province or region (but not the city or town)
      in which the center is located?   _____
   c. Outside the province or region?   _____

E.3. Job Placement and Follow-up

1. Are graduates helped to find employment?   ☐Y ☐N
2. If yes,
    a. Does the school or training center operate a
       placement service?   ☐Y ☐N
    b. Does the ministry of labor arrange placement?   ☐Y ☐N
    c. What other help is given? (Specify.) _____
       _____
3. If yes to (2a), what services are provided? (Describe
   briefly.) _____
4. a. What percentage of graduates or trainees is in
      jobs within six months?   75 ☐ 50 ☐ 25 ☐ 10 ☐
   b. Within one year?   75 ☐ 50 ☐ 25 ☐ 10 ☐
5. In which trades is it easiest to place graduates?
   (1 indicates easiest.)
       1. _____
       2. _____
       3. _____
6. In which trades is it most difficult for graduates to
   obtain employment? (1 indicates most difficult.)
       1. _____
       2. _____
       3. _____
7. Is there a follow-up service?   ☐Y ☐N
8. If yes,
    a. For how many years after graduation?   _____
    b. What is the frequency of follow-up?   _____
9. Is there a special budget for placement and follow-
   up services?   ☐Y ☐N

E.4. Staff Selection and Promotion

1. What are the minimum criteria for appointment as assistant instructor?
   a. General education (how many years?)
   b. Technical education or vocational training (how many years?)
   c. Technical teacher training course (state length)
   d. Trade experience (how many years?)
   e. Practical test before appointment
   f. Satisfactory personal interview
   g. Medical
   h. Age (specify)

E.5. Staff Development Plans

1. What is the basis for determining the number and
   type of instructors?
   a. Hours or periods of teaching required in each
      subject or specialization ☐
   b. Student-staff ratio, by course or training program ☐
   c. Student-staff ratio, for center as a whole ☐
   d. Combination of (a), (b), and (c) ☐
2. What is the nominal weekly teaching duty in periods
   (give length) or in hours? _____
3. What is the present average weekly teaching duty
   for all staff, in hours? _____
4. If (3) differs from (2), explain. _____
5. Is there a staff development plan?   Y N
6. If yes, does the plan include arrangements for
   a. Technical upgrading?   Y N
   b. Teacher training?   Y N
      Pre-service   Y N
      In-service   Y N
   c. Management training for senior staff?   Y N
7. If yes to (5), is the plan adequate?   Y N
8. If yes to (5), is there a regular review of
   implementation of the plan?   Y N
9. Is there a budget for staff development?   Y N

E.6. External and Industrial Activities

1. Does the center provide any training programs
   designed jointly with a firm for that firm's employees?   Y   N
2. If yes, give details of the nature, length, and
   frequency of that program and the number trained.
3. Does the center provide any support—technical,
   financial, or the use of its facilities—for graduates who
   are self-employed entrepreneurs?   Y   N
4. If yes, describe. _____
5. Does the center provide any technical or other
   support to local industry?   Y   N
6. If yes, describe the nature and amount of such support. _____
7. Does the center or school undertake production
   activities or provide services other than training for
   which it receives income?   Y   N
8. If yes, list the products or services, the amount of
   production or activity, and the value or income.

Product or service	Output (physical units, or hours of service)	Value or income

9. If yes to (7), describe staff and trainee involvement in the activity. _____
_____

E.7. Management

Responsibilities

Instructions: For each of the following, check Y if the school is directly responsible for that activity. If N is checked, indicate the body (for example, a central ministry or a regional office of a ministry) that is responsible.

a. Recruitment and appointment of teaching staff   Y☐ N☐ _____

b. Recruitment and appointment of support staff   Y☐ N☐ _____

c. Recruitment or selection of students   Y☐ N☐ _____

d. Design of curricula and syllabuses   Y☐ N☐ _____

e. Adaptation of curricula and syllabuses to local conditions   Y☐ N☐ _____

f. Revision of curricula and syllabuses   Y☐ N☐ _____

g. Preparation of teaching and training materials   Y☐ N☐ _____

h. Design of examinations   Y☐ N☐ _____

i. Marking of examinations or tests   Y☐ N☐ _____

j. Purchase of equipment   Y☐ N☐ _____

k. Purchase of consumable materials   Y☐ N☐ _____

Coordination with Local Industry

a. Is there an advisory body?   Y☐ N☐

b. How often does it meet? _____

c. In what areas is it active? _____

Instructor Staff

a. Do instructors work as a team?   Y☐ N☐

b. Are there senior instructors or heads of department with responsibility for all courses in their trade?   Y☐ N☐

c. Are duties and terms of reference of staff given in writing?   Y☐ N☐

d. How often are staff meetings held? _____

Organization

a. Does the center operate on single, double, or triple shifts (specify)?

b. Is there a center timetable for the year?   Y☐ N☐

c. Is there a workshop loading chart?   Y☐ N☐

d. Are there individual staff teaching timetables?   Y☐ N☐

e. During what hours (or periods) is the center open each week? _____

f. How many weeks each year does the center operate? _____

Records

a. Does the center have records of trainee selection
   and admission? [Y] [N]
b. Are attendance registers maintained? [Y] [N]
c. Is there a chart or other method of monitoring
   trainee progress? [Y] [N]
d. Are records kept of trainee performance in trade
   tests or other examinations? [Y] [N]
e. Are records kept of trainees' careers after
   graduation? [Y] [N]
f. Are records kept of instructors' qualifications and
   experience? [Y] [N]
g. Are records kept on instructors' and trainees'
   absences? [Y] [N]
h. Are records kept on training taken by instructors? [Y] [N]
i. Are the following teaching records available for
   examination?
      Curricula [Y] [N]
      Course programs [Y] [N]
      Lesson plans [Y] [N]
      Instruction or job sheets [Y] [N]
j. Are the following financial records available for
   examination?
      Teaching staff salaries [Y] [N]
      Support staff salaries [Y] [N]
      Expenditure on consumable materials [Y] [N]
      Maintenance costs of buildings and equipment [Y] [N]
      Consumption and cost of electricity, gas, and other
        services [Y] [N]
      Taxes paid [Y] [N]

Equipment, Spare Tools, and Consumable Materials

a. Is an inventory of equipment and materials
   maintained? [Y] [N]
b. What is the system for controlling use of materials from stores? _____
   _____
c. What is the procedure for purchasing imported items—equipment, spare parts,
   and materials? _____
d. What is the procedure for purchasing locally made items or local materials?
   _____

Accounting

a. Are accounts comprehensive and up to date? [Y] [N]
b. Are costs analyzed to give costs per trainee or per
   graduate? [Y] [N]
c. Are comparative costs used as a management tool? [Y] [N]

Name of school or center _____

E.8. Teaching Activities Observed

Instructions: Complete for each class or course observed. Y, yes; N, no; E, excellent; G, good; F, fair; P, poor.

| Skill or speciali-zation | Curriculum | | Teaching methods used | | | | | Teaching materials used | | Teaching aids used | | | Performance evaluation | |
	Course program available	Lesson plan available	Notes dictated to students	Notes copied from black-board	Group demonstration	Individual instruction	Programmed instruction	Instruction sheets	Information sheets	Audio-visual	Charts	Models	Quality of trainees' work	Quality of instruction
1.	Y N	Y N	Y N	Y N	Y N	Y N	Y N	Y N	Y N	Y N	Y N	Y N	E G F P	E G F P
2.	Y N	Y N	Y N	Y N	Y N	Y N	Y N	Y N	Y N	Y N	Y N	Y N	E G F P	E G F P
3.	Y N	Y N	Y N	Y N	Y N	Y N	Y N	Y N	Y N	Y N	Y N	Y N	E G F P	E G F P
4.	Y N	Y N	Y N	Y N	Y N	Y N	Y N	Y N	Y N	Y N	Y N	Y N	E G F P	E G F P
5.	Y N	Y N	Y N	Y N	Y N	Y N	Y N	Y N	Y N	Y N	Y N	Y N	E G F P	E G F P
6.	Y N	Y N	Y N	Y N	Y N	Y N	Y N	Y N	Y N	Y N	Y N	Y N	E G F P	E G F P
7.	Y N	Y N	Y N	Y N	Y N	Y N	Y N	Y N	Y N	Y N	Y N	Y N	E G F P	E G F P
8.	Y N	Y N	Y N	Y N	Y N	Y N	Y N	Y N	Y N	Y N	Y N	Y N	E G F P	E G F P
9.	Y N	Y N	Y N	Y N	Y N	Y N	Y N	Y N	Y N	Y N	Y N	Y N	E G F P	E G F P
10.	Y N	Y N	Y N	Y N	Y N	Y N	Y N	Y N	Y N	Y N	Y N	Y N	E G F P	E G F P

Name of school or center _____

E.9. Quality of Teaching Materials and of Training Programs

Instructions: Complete for each class or course for which materials were inspected. E, excellent; G, good; F, fair; P, poor.

Skill or specialization	Format of curricula and syllabuses				Teaching materials		Evaluation of quality of teaching material
	By topic or subject, without description of treatment	By topic or subject, with description of treatment	Based on learning or behavioral objectives		Teachers' notes with description of treatment	Students' notes, or training materials for self-paced work	
			Course-based, nonmodular	Modular			
1.	Yes No	Yes No	Yes No	Yes No	Yes No	Yes No	E G F P
2.	Yes No	Yes No	Yes No	Yes No	Yes No	Yes No	E G F P
3.	Yes No	Yes No	Yes No	Yes No	Yes No	Yes No	E G F P
4.	Yes No	Yes No	Yes No	Yes No	Yes No	Yes No	E G F P
5.	Yes No	Yes No	Yes No	Yes No	Yes No	Yes No	E G F P
6.	Yes No	Yes No	Yes No	Yes No	Yes No	Yes No	E G F P
7.	Yes No	Yes No	Yes No	Yes No	Yes No	Yes No	E G F P
8.	Yes No	Yes No	Yes No	Yes No	Yes No	Yes No	E G F P
9.	Yes No	Yes No	Yes No	Yes No	Yes No	Yes No	E G F P
10.	Yes No	Yes No	Yes No	Yes No	Yes No	Yes No	E G F P

Name of school or center _____

E.10. Upkeep of Laboratories and Workshops

Instructions: Complete for each class or course observed. Number of trainees and instructors are those at time of visit. E, excellent; G, good; F, fair; P, poor.

Work-shop	Number of trainees	Number of instruc-tors	Structural condition: roof, walls, floors, windows	Condition of paint: walls, windows, doors	Cleanliness of floors, walls, machinery	Internal order: trainees, work flow, equip-ment	Electrical installa-tions: fuses, boxes	Safety and protection	First aid and fire equipment	Light-ing	Ventila-tion, tempera-ture	Overall assessment
1.			E G F P	E G F P	E G F P	E G F P	E G F P	E G F P	E G F P	E G F P	E G F P	E G F P
2.			E G F P	E G F P	E G F P	E G F P	E G F P	E G F P	E G F P	E G F P	E G F P	E G F P
3.			E G F P	E G F P	E G F P	E G F P	E G F P	E G F P	E G F P	E G F P	E G F P	E G F P
4.			E G F P	E G F P	E G F P	E G F P	E G F P	E G F P	E G F P	E G F P	E G F P	E G F P
5.			E G F P	E G F P	E G F P	E G F P	E G F P	E G F P	E G F P	E G F P	E G F P	E G F P
6.			E G F P	E G F P	E G F P	E G F P	E G F P	E G F P	E G F P	E G F P	E G F P	E G F P
7.			E G F P	E G F P	E G F P	E G F P	E G F P	E G F P	E G F P	E G F P	E G F P	E G F P
8.			E G F P	E G F P	E G F P	E G F P	E G F P	E G F P	E G F P	E G F P	E G F P	E G F P
9.			E G F P	E G F P	E G F P	E G F P	E G F P	E G F P	E G F P	E G F P	E G F P	E G F P
10.			E G F P	E G F P	E G F P	E G F P	E G F P	E G F P	E G F P	E G F P	E G F P	E G F P

Name of school or center _____

E.11. Utilization of Equipment

Instructions: Complete for each laboratory or workshop inspected.

| Laboratory or workshop (1) | What percentage of equipment is | | If answer to (3) is less than 70 percent, this is because of | | | | | | Is there a regular scheme for recording utilization of equipment? | | Is there a regular maintenance program? | | Give details of any major problems with utilization of equipment |
	In good working order (2)	Used regularly (25 hours or more a week)	Shortage of materials	Lack of spare parts	Lack of instruments	Inappropriate equipment	Obsolete equipment	Other	Yes	No	Yes	No	

Name of school or center _____

E.12. Availability and Use of Small Tools and Measuring Equipment

a. Is there an adequate stock of small tools and
   measuring equipment?   Y N

b. Are the small tools and measuring equipment in
   regular use?   Y N

c. Are they well maintained and serviceable?   Y N

d. Are the tool cupboards or tool stores well organized? Y N

e. Is there a system for controlling inflow and outflow
   of tools and equipment to trainees?   Y N

f. Is there a storekeeper?   Y N

g. If no, is the instructor responsible?   Y N

h. If no to (7), is a trainee designated as storekeeper? Y N

i. Are worn-out and broken tools and equipment
   replaced without delay?   Y N

Name of school or center _____

E.13. Availability and Use of Consumable Materials

Note: Consumable materials are materials, such as metals, wood, building materials, welding rods, electric components, and paper, that are used in training. Small tools and instruments that have a working life of less than two years may also be included.

a. What is the approximate annual expenditure on consumable materials for each area or specialization for the past two years?

Skill area or specialization (list)	*Expenditure for consumable materials (local currency)*	
	198_/__	*198_/__*

Total expenditure

b. Who determines annual expenditures? _____
c. Who selects the materials to be purchased? _____
d. How long does it normally take to procure materials? _____
e. Is the store well organized? _____
f. Is the storekeeper trained? _____
g. What records are kept on use of materials? _____

Name of school or center _____

E.14. Questionnaire for Instructors

Instructions: This questionnaire is designed as a basis for an interview with a small group of instructors (about six to eight). The answers should record the consensus (if there is one) or indicate the diversity of views.

1. What course(s) do you teach?
2. In your opinion, are there enough instructors for the vocational program?
   a. Enough
   b. Too few
   c. No opinion
3. If there are too few instructors, what is the main reason?
   a. Pay is too low
   b. There is no interest in the speciality
   c. Other
4. What is your main reason for entering the teaching profession?
   a. Money
   b. Status or social position
   c. Good working conditions
   d. Employment stability
5. If you have colleagues who have left the teaching profession, what were the main reasons?
   a. Too few chances for promotion
   b. Mental fatigue or stress
   c. Pay too low
   d. Working conditions bad
   e. Duties too heavy
6. What is the range of class size in your courses?   _____
   Do you think this number is
   a. Adequate?
   b. Too large?
   c. Too small?
   d. No opinion
7. In your opinion, what is the level of the students' ability in relation to the planned level of the course?
   a. Superior
   b. Inferior
   c. The same
8. In your opinion, what is the main reason for students' dropping out?
   a. Inadequate level of knowledge
   b. Difficulty of travel to center or school
   c. Lack of discipline
   d. Health
   e. Financial reasons
   f. Availability of employment before graduation
   g. Family problems
   h. Other

9. Do you have enough teaching materials for your courses?
   a. Yes
   b. No
   c. Satisfactory in some ways, but not in others (give details)
10. Is the equipment adequate for your courses?
    a. Yes
    b. Insufficient in quantity
    c. Inadequate in quality or range
    d. Technologically obsolete
11. Is the equipment similar to that used in industry?
    a. Similar
    b. Superior
    c. Inferior
12. What do you think of the maintenance and cleanliness of workshops?
    a. Good
    b. Insufficient
13. In your opinion, is it easy for graduates to obtain employment?
    a. Easy
    b. Difficult
    c. Don't know
14. If it is difficult, what is the main reason?
    a. There is little demand for the specialty.
    b. The training is inadequate.
    c. Other (give details)
15. In your opinion, what two measures would contribute most to the improvement of the school or center?
    a. Improve buildings
    b. Provide more equipment
    c. Review and update curricula
    d. Improve materials
    e. Upgrade instructors
    f. Improve student selection
    g. Improve counseling and placement of graduates
    h. Coordinate courses more closely with the requirements of the market

Name of school or center _____

E.15. Questionnaire for Students or Trainees

Instructions: This questionnaire is designed as a basis for an interview with a small group of students or trainees (about six to eight). The answers should record the consensus (if there is one) or indicate the diversity of views.

1. What courses are you taking? (Record all courses mentioned.)

2. What were your main reasons for enrolling in the course?
   a. My employer is sponsoring me.
   b. I am unemployed or am a school leaver and want to improve my job prospects.
   c. I want to start my own business.
   d. I was not accepted in a course I preferred (give details).
   e. I want to learn a skill.
   f. Other

3. What do you think will be your chance of employment at the end of the course?
   a. Good
   b. Fair
   c. Poor
   d. Other

4. What is your opinion of the course, compared with your expectations?
   a. It meets my needs and expectations.
   b. I am disappointed by the course.
   c. If (b), give reasons.

5. In your opinion, which of the following aspects of the course are satisfactory or unsatisfactory? (S, satisfactory, U, unsatisfactory, ?, no opinion).
   a. Level of training [S] [U] [?]
   b. Content of training [S] [U] [?]
   c. Number of instructors [S] [U] [?]
   d. Quality of instructors [S] [U] [?]
   e. Laboratory or workshop equipment [S] [U] [?]
   f. Exercises in laboratories or workshops [S] [U] [?]
   g. Discipline [S] [U] [?]
   h. Other aspects (specify) [S] [U] [?]

6. What is the average class size in your courses?
   a. Theory class   _____
   b. Laboratory or workshop   _____
   For theory class, is this number
   a. Adequate?
   b. Too large?
   c. Too small?
   For laboratory or workshop, is this number
   a. Adequate?
   b. Too large?
   c. Too small?
7. In your opinion what is the level of training in the course in relation to the ability of the students? For theory course,
   a. Course too difficult
   b. Course too easy
   c. Level about right
   For laboratory or workshop,
   a. Course too difficult
   b. Course too easy
   c. Level about right
8. In your opinion, what is the main reason for students' dropping out?
   a. Course too difficult
   b. Difficulty of travel to center or school
   c. Lack of discipline
   d. Health
   e. Financial reasons
   f. Employment available before graduation
   g. Family problems
   h. Other
9. Do you consider that you have received adequate guidance
   a. About the course or training?   Y N
   b. About job availability?   Y N
   c. About other possible careers?   Y N
10. In your opinion, what two actions would most improve the course(s)?
    a. Improve buildings
    b. Improve equipment
    c. Raise standard of training staff
    d. Raise standard of course
    e. Increase length of course
    f. Provide better guidance to trainees before course
    g. Tighten discipline

11. Do you consider your views to be representative
    of all students?   Y   N
    If no, give details.

External Efficiency: Sample Questionnaires

F.1. Questionnaire for Employers

Instructions: Check appropriate box or supply information requested.

Name of company _____
Industry _____
Number of workers   50–200 ☐   200–500 ☐   more than 500 ☐
This questionnaire refers only to skilled workers and higher-skilled workers or craftsmen.

1. Approximately how many workers in these occupations did you hire last year?

	Skilled workers	*Higher-skilled workers*
a. Less than 10	☐	☐
b. 10–20	☐	☐
c. 20–30	☐	☐
d. 30–40	☐	☐
e. 50–100	☐	☐
f. 100–200	☐	☐
g. 200–300	☐	☐
h. More than 300	☐	☐

2. Can you easily get workers in these occupations?
    a. Skilled   ☐Y ☐N
    b. Higher-skilled   ☐Y ☐N
3. If yes, do they have the type of training you would like to see in your workers?
    a. Skilled   ☐Y ☐N
    b. Higher-skilled   ☐Y ☐N
4. If you answered no to (2) or (3), what do you do?
    a. Offer higher wages to attract better workers from other firms ☐
    b. Offer higher wages to attract new graduates ☐
    c. Offer more fringe benefits ☐
    d. Accept less qualified candidates ☐
    e. Other ☐

5. If you answered (a), (b), or (c), how much higher? or what extra fringe benefits?
   a. 10 percent   ☐
   b. 20 percent   ☐
   c. 30 percent   ☐
   d. Type of fringe benefits   _____

6. How do you recruit new workers?
   a. Advertise in newspapers   ☐
   b. Use word-of-mouth of employed workers   ☐
   c. Contact vocational schools   ☐
   d. Contact training institutes and skill-training centers   ☐
   e. Provide own training   ☐
   f. Other   ☐

7. How many applicants do you get for each job opening?
   a. Skilled workers   _____
   b. Higher-skilled workers   _____

8. Which of the following criteria do you use when hiring new workers? (Choose the two most important ones.)
   a. References from former employers   ☐
   b. References from other workers   ☐
   c. References from vocational schools   ☐
   d. References from institutes and training centers   ☐
   e. Evaluation of vocational school grades   ☐
   f. Examination and practical tests at the plant   ☐
   g. Other   ☐

9. Which candidate of those described below is most likely to be hired?

	Skilled workers	*Higher-skilled workers*
a. Middle school with skill-center training	☐	☐
b. Middle school with one year's experience	☐	☐
c. Technical vocational high school with no experience	☐	☐
d. Academic high school with one year's experience	☐	☐

10. Why do you prefer your choices? (Choose the two more important reasons for each.)

	Skilled workers	Higher-skilled workers
a. They have more theoretical knowledge.	☐	☐
b. They have more practical knowledge.	☐	☐
c. They have more theoretical and practical knowledge.	☐	☐
d. They have more initiative.	☐	☐
e. They are more productive immediately.	☐	☐
f. They can advance faster into higher skills.	☐	☐
g. They are more reliable.	☐	☐
h. They follow instructions better.	☐	☐
i. Their starting salary is lower.	☐	☐

11. Even though candidates seem to have the background you prefer, you probably reject some before hiring one. How many of the same background do you usually reject before hiring one worker?
    a. Skilled workers   _____
    b. Higher-skilled workers   _____

12. In general, why are candidates rejected?

	Skilled workers	Higher-skilled workers
a. They lack theoretical knowledge.	☐	☐
b. They lack practical knowledge.	☐	☐
c. They lack the proper attitude.	☐	☐
d. They ask too much money.	☐	☐
e. They lack theoretical and practical knowledge.	☐	☐

13. When you hire workers without experience, how do you train them?
    a. Foremen and other skilled persons show them how to work. ☐
    b. We provide special in-plant training. ☐
    c. We sponsor training in skill centers or vocational training institutes. ☐

14. Have you hired graduates from vocational high schools (skill centers), in the past few years? Ⓨ Ⓝ

15. If yes, how do you rate the graduates of technical high schools (skill centers) compared with workers in the same occupation but with different educational backgrounds?

	Skilled workers	Higher-skilled workers
a. They are the same as other workers.	☐	☐
b. They are better.	☐	☐
c. They are not as good.	☐	☐
d. No opinion	☐	☐

16. If you answered that they are not as good, why?

	Skilled workers	Higher-skilled workers
a. They lack theoretical knowledge.	☐	☐
b. They lack practical knowledge.	☐	☐
c. They are not acquainted with the machinery in the plant.	☐	☐
d. They lack discipline.	☐	☐
e. Other _____	☐	☐

17. If you answered that they are as good or better, do the graduates usually demand higher wages than other applicants? [Y] [N]

    By how much (percent)?   10 ☐ 20 ☐ 30 ☐ more ☐

18. Are you familiar with the vocational school (skill center)? [Y] [N]

19. If so, what is your opinion of it?
    a. Good   ☐
    b. Average   ☐
    c. Poor   ☐
    d. No opinion ☐

F.2. Questionnaire for Employees

Instructions: This questionnaire is designed as a basis for an interview with a small group of employees (about six to eight). The interview should record the consensus, if there is one, or indicate the diversity of views.

If it is not possible to administer a questionnaire to employees, find out whether employers can provide individual records on relevant employees. These might include occupation, sex, age, education, training, and earnings.

Name of company _____

Industry _____

Number of workers   50–200 ☐   200–500 ☐   more than 500 ☐

Name of employee _____

1. Occupation
2. Age
    a. 16–18
    b. 19–21
    c. 22–25
    d. 26 and older
3. Level of formal schooling before entering training program
    a. Primary school
    b. Middle school
    c. Academic high school
4. Type of training program
    a. Technical high school
    b. Training in skill center
    c. On-the-job training in industry
    d. Apprenticeship
    e. Other _____
5. Type of program
    a. Mechanical
    b. Chemical
    c. Electrical
    d. Electronics
    e. Other
6. Length of training program
    a. 1–6 months
    b. 7–12 months
    c. 13–18 months
    d. 19–24 months
    e. 25–36 months
7. Year when graduated from formal school   _____
8. Year when graduated from (or finished) training   _____
9. Is this your first job?   Y N
10. If no, what occupation did you have before this one?   _____

11. How long did it take you to find a job after training?
    a. I found a job immediately.
    b. 3 months
    c. 6 months
    d. 9 months
    e. 1 year
    f. More than a year
12. How much do you earn now?   _____
13. How much did you earn last year?   _____
    How much did you earn the year before last?   _____
14. When you graduated, did you expect to earn
    a. More than now?
    b. Less than now?
    c. About the same?
    d. Don't know
15. Is your present occupation related to your training?   ☐Y ☐N
16. If no, why?
    a. I did not find work in the occupation for which
       I trained.
    b. I did not wish to work in the occupation for which
       I trained.
17. What type of knowledge do you think is primarily
    needed for performing efficiently in your job?
    a. Theoretical
    b. Practical
    c. Experience
    d. Theoretical and practical
    e. Theoretical and experience
    f. Practical and experience
18. Are you applying in your work what you learned
    during your training?
    a. No
    b. A little
    c. A lot
19. If you answered (b) or (c), of all the things you
    learned in your training, what is the one thing that
    is most useful for your work?
    a. Use of machinery
    b. Theoretical instruction
    c. Advice of teachers
20. In your work, are you using equipment similar to
    that used during your training?   ☐Y ☐N
21. Was what you learned during your training enough
    to enable you to perform successfully on your job?   ☐Y ☐N

22. If no, why?
    a. Training did not provide experience.
    b. Training did not provide practical knowledge.
    c. Training did not provide theoretical knowledge.
    d. Training did not provide practical or theoretical knowledge.
    e. Training was too short.
    f. Training was too long.
    g. Other
23. Did some of your co-workers go through the same type of training as you did?   Y N
24. If yes, what is your opinion of their capacities compared with co-workers who did not go through the same type of training?
    a. They are better workers.
    b. They are not as good.
    c. They are equally good.
    d. Don't know.
25a. If the answer was (a), why are they better?
    a. They have more knowledge.
    b. They have more experience.
    c. They are more responsible.
    d. They behave better.
25b. If you consider your training mates less capable than other workers, why is that so?
    a. Other workers have more knowledge.
    b. Other workers have more experience.
    c. Other workers are more responsible.
    d. Other workers behave better.
26. Do you think having gone through your particular type of training has paid off?   Y N Don't know ☐
27. If you think it has paid off, why?
    a. I got a good job.
    b. I am earning more money than without the training.
    c. I have more prestige than somebody without my training.
    d. It opened up possibilities for employment and advancement.
28. If you don't think it has paid off, why?
    a. I didn't get a good job.
    b. I am not earning more than I would have earned otherwise.
    c. I have little status at work.
    d. It did not open up possibilities for advancement.

29. How did you get your job?
   a. Through school placement
   b. Through friends
   c. Through newspaper ads
   d. Through an employment agency
   e. Other
29. Would you recommend to your friends or relatives
   the same type of training you took?   Y N